The Chameleon

Handbook

François Le Berre

Filled with color photos

BARRON'S

Dedication

To Tonton Andre. Life is a continuum, just as much as a relay race.

About the Author

François Le Berre is a Naturalist born in Montreal who grew up in Africa. As a child, he had an encounter with a Senegal's chameleon that gave the kick-start to a lifelong dedicated study of this group of lizards. He currently works and lives in Asia.

Photo Credits

Sebastien Butez: page 72; Wolfgang Schmidt: page 71; Dave Weldon: pages 89, 90, 92, and 93. All other photographs were taken by François Le Berre.

Cover Credits

Front cover, back cover, inside front cover, inside back cover: Shutterstock.

All inquiries should be addressed to:
Barron's Educational Series, Inc.
250 Wireless Boulevard
Hauppauge, New York 11788
www.barronseduc.com

ISBN-10: 0-7641-4142-2
ISBN-13: 978-0-7641-4142-3

Library of Congress Control Number: 2008939528

Printed in China

9 8 7 6

Important Note

Before using any of the electrical equipment described in this book, be sure to read "Avoiding Electrical Accidents" on page 71.

While handling chameleons you may occasionally receive bites or scratches. If your skin is broken, see your physician immediately.

Some terrarium plants may be harmful to the skin or mucous membranes of human beings. If you notice any signs of irritation, wash the area thoroughly. See your physician if the condition persists.

Chameleons may transmit certain infections to humans. Always wash your hands carefully after handling your specimens. Always supervise children who wish to observe your chameleons.

Contents

PART TWO: CHAMELEONS UNDER HUMAN CARE

Preface

A bit over a decade has passed since the first edition of *The New Chameleon Handbook* and what a difference a decade makes! Fifteen years ago, the information we dreamed of getting on chameleons was incredibly scarce and hard to obtain. The biology and the life history of most of the chameleon species were shrouded in a veil of mystery. Chameleons were the "impossible-to-keep-no-need-to-try" type of lizard, better left to themselves in the wildernesses of Africa or the jungles of Madagascar. And if we had bowed to the dark opinions of the skeptics, that's where they would have remained.

Chameleons, "color changing dragons" to the Chinese, and "tree dragons" to the Westerners have often been endowed with supranatural abilities in the African and Malagasy folklore. Arboreal lizards with an uncanny ability for stealth or appearance, they are considered by many of these cultures to be the messengers of an ethereal world on Earth. If there were a message to be received, it would be in my opinion, that we are very much like chameleons ourselves, a bridge between two worlds. The human species is the only one with the power to consciously modify its environment, and it is this that makes us humans. Bringing other life forms into our world and disseminating them is also a means to connect with a natural world from which we seem to distance ourselves from more and more.

This book never would have existed without passion: your passion and that of so many others, which fueled and rejuvenated my own. You who inspired me and gave me the desire to spend more time and effort trying to understand these beloved creatures, this book—as a testimony, a celebration, and an invitation—is my offering to you.

Calumma parsonii var. cristifer.

Introduction

This book is a short, quick introduction to a vast and fascinating subject: chameleons. It is not intended to explain everything, nor does it expect the reader to be a chameleon expert (but if you are, you have my congratulations!). It is meant to provide guidance, to give you a feeling for the animals, and to fuel your interest in them. As with training in other fields, deep knowledge of chameleons comes only with long years of study, travel, observation, and experience. The reader should, however, gain through this book a keener awareness of chameleons—their life and biology, their needs and habits—as well as useful knowledge for designing enclosures, chameleon breeding, and living in harmony with the chameleon world.

If there were a few things to keep in mind when working with chameleons, I would term them as being physiological and psychological needs. On a physiological part, most chameleons thrive on a certain volume of private space with mild temperatures, slightly high relative humidity, access to sunlight, and live food rich in antioxidants. On the psychological part, chameleons need to have a sense of security and respect from their keeper. They are particularly sensitive animals that must be treated with care and deference, keeping in mind that in the chameleon world, patience is godly.

What do you get from keeping chameleons? The obvious answer is: a lot of joy, and a probable ticket to another world, the world of Chameleons!

Calumma Fallax *(male)*.

PART ONE
EXPLORATION OF THE CHAMELEON REALM

Chapter One
What Are Chameleons?

Chameleons are a group of old-world, slow-moving, carnivorous lizards, with an insectivorous specialization and a unique morphology (form) among lizards. Of their numerous extraordinary physical features (projectile tongue, turreted independently swiveling eyes, and an uncanny ability for both extravagant colors and stealth), none is more unique in the reptile kingdom than their feet, with their parrot-like opposable toes, which are meant not just to grip, but to seize.

Chameleon Diversity

If a chameleon in the mind of the general public looks like a green, leaf-shaped lizard a bit like the Gracile's chameleon (*Chamaeleo gracilis*), chameleons in reality are a diverse group of almost 180 species and subspecies, and among which color variations, sizes, and adornments are staggering. Half of the chameleon species known to the world to date live in Madagascar, the largest island of the Mascarenes (which also include the Seychelles, Comoros, La Réunion, Mauritius, Anjouan, and Mayotte) off the coast of Mozambique. The second-richest area in chameleon species is East Africa, the third is South Africa, and the fourth is Equatorial Africa. Many species are intimately linked to very specific habitats called biomes and are dependant on the microclimates they find there for their survival.

Species, Subspecies, and Variations

A species is a group of individuals exhibiting the same characteristics, living in the same habitat, and able to breed among themselves to produce fertile young. Species are sometimes further divided into subspecies and variations or morphs.

A subspecies is a population geographically isolated from the parental population and presenting specific genetic characteristics that differ from the species type. Successful breeding between subspecies is possible.

Variations usually indicate a geographical color morph, which are quite common in chameleons. One of the best examples of this is the

1

Chamaeleo jacksonii xantholophus *(male).*

Panther chameleon (*Furcifer pardalis*), for which more than 12 color morphs referring to locales where they are found are already known.

Classifying Chameleons

Researchers who have an interest in the classification of life forms (sorting out the different groups) are called systematists or taxonomists. Some of these biologists differ in their complex rules and methods of classification and thus distinguish themselves as either *Linnaean taxonomists* or *phylogenetic systematists*.

All biologists, however, follow Linnaeus's binomial classification system. Under this system, each life form is given a unique scientific name in Latin, made up of its genus name and its species name, to differentiate it from any other life form.

For example, the Veiled chameleon is also commonly called the Yemen chameleon after its country of origin, which can lead to confusion about the species in question. Scientists, on the other hand, refer to this particular chameleon by its scientific name, *Chamaeleo calyptratus*, to ensure that they are talking about the same animal.

Biologists study life from the very broad (ecosystems) to the smallest unit (cells), and their hierarchic classification system also goes from the general to the particular. In their view, each chameleon fits into something bigger than itself: the history of the species, a chameleon population, a species as an entity, or an ecosystem, to name a few possibilities. Using this system, the established population of Jackson's chameleons found on the Hawaiian islands of Holualoa and Maui can be classified as described in the table on page 3.

Two Views of Chameleon Taxonomy

Linnaean taxonomy relies on morphological similarities (hemipenis and lung structures in the case of typical chameleons) as a means to classify living beings. Molecular phylogenetics (also called cladistics), on the other hand, makes use of molecular biology, DNA and RNA study, and evolutionary processes to chart the tree of life. The emergence of powerful computers, genetic research, and other technologies has given an edge to molecular phy-

Taxonomy of *Chamaeleo (Trioceros) jacksonii xantholophus*

Kingdom: Animalia—Animal

Phylum: Chordata—Vertebrate, an animal with a backbone

Class: Reptilia—Reptile, the group containing squamata; some taxonomists might also include in it chelonians (terrapins, soft-shelled turtles, marine turtles, and land tortoises), crocodilians (crocodiles, alligators, caimans, and gavials), and sphenodontids (tuataras)

Order: Squamata—The group containing snakes, amphisbaenas, and lizards

Suborder: Sauria—Lizard

Family: Chamaeleonidae—Typical and stump-tailed chameleons

Subfamily: Chamaeleoninae—Chamaeleonid (with the physical features common to chameleons)

Genus: *Chamaeleo*—African chameleon group

Subgenus: *Trioceros*—Three-horned chameleon group

Species: *jacksonii*—"Jackson's chameleon," named after Sir Jackson

Subspecies: *xantholophus*—Yellow-crested Jackson's chameleon

logenetics. Both taxonomic continue to evolve, accounting for the ever-changing classifications of the genera and species we will cover. This should not be a cause of confusion. In cladistics, a clade (group of species) might radiate to new clades (generally because of ecological factors, such as climate change or habitat change), but these clades might continue to coexist and show strong similarities millions of years later. Since molecular phylogenetics is based on the DNA study of the animals and not on their physical aspects, it splits clades more readily into different genera.

Chameleon Genera

In phylogenetics, chameleons are covered under a common clade, Acrodonta, and divided into nine genera, which may also comprise subgenera.

Bradypodion (from the Latinized Greek *bradus podos*, "slow foot") Fitzinger, 1843, live-bearing South African dwarf chameleons

Calumma Gray, 1865, Madagascan chameleons with occipital lobes

Furcifer pardalis *(males) Ambanja and Sambava morph.*

Furcifer pardalis *(male) Nosy Faly morph.*

Chamaeleo (from the Latinized Greek *Kamaii leon,* "small lion"), Laurenti, 1768, African Chameleons, comprising subgenus *Chamaeleo* and subgenus *Trioceros*), excluding *Chamaeleo namaquensis*

Furcifer (from the Latin, furci, "forked," referring to the feet), Fitzinger, 1834, Madagascan chameleons, excluding *Furcifer balteatus*

Kinyongia (from the Swahili name for chameleons, *Kinyonga*), Tilbury, Tolley, and Branch, 2006, comprises some East African chameleons

Nadzikambia Tilbury, Tolley, Branch, and Matthee, 2006, currently comprised of only one species from East Africa: *Nadzikambia mlanjense*

Brookesia (named after the British naturalist Brookes), Gray, 1865, Madagascan stump-tailed chameleons, possibly excluding *Brookesia nasus*

Rieppeleon (named after the scientist Olivier Rieppel), Matthee, Tilbury, and Townsend, 2004, East African pigmy leaf chameleons with no rostral horns

Furcifer pardalis *(male) Ambilobe morph.*

Rhampholeon (from the Latinized Greek *ramphos* leon, "crawling lion") Guenther, 1874, West and Central African pygmy leaf chameleons with a nasal appendage, comprising the subgenera *Rhinodigitum, Biscuspis,* and *Rhampholeon*

The Two Chameleon Subfamilies: Chameleoninae and Brookesinae

For hobbyists, chameleons fit in either one of two groups: stump-tailed or pygmy leaf chameleons and true chameleons. In fact, the family Chamaeleonidae, which contains all chameleons, consists of just these two subfamilies. Specifically, the "true" (or typical) chameleons and the South African dwarf chameleons belong to the subfamily Chameleoninae; the stump-tailed chameleons are members of the subfamily Brookesinae.

Note: To simplify things, when discussing any members of this family, I will use the term *chameleon*, or

chamaeleonids. If additional clarification is necessary, I will refer to members of *Calumma, Chamaeleo, Furcifer, Kinyongia, and Nadzikambia* as typical chameleons. The term South African dwarf chameleons will be used for South African members of *Bradypodion.* Stump-tailed

Furcifer pardalis *(male) Ambilobe red morph.*

chameleons refers to all members of the subfamily Brookesinae, *Brookesia*, *Rieppeleon*, and *Rhampholeon* alike.

External Morphology

As with all lizards, the body of chameleons is covered with a scaly skin, more or less permeable to water. Chameleons have prehensile tails varying in length. Just like the inner side of chameleons' feet, their tails are adorned with specialized conical pads for a better grip. The pads can be felt by gently running a finger on the underside of a chameleon's tail. What is not lizard-like in chameleons, however, is their ears, which have simplified with evolution and are not externally visible.

Gender Differences

Most chameleons show sexual differences (sexual dimorphism). Often, males have secondary characteristics such as horns and vertebral and/or caudal crests, as seen in the Mountain chameleon (*Chamaeleo montium)*.

Gender-related morphology and/or color differences (sexual dichromatism) occur in most species. In species that do not exhibit overt sexual differences, such as *Chamaeleo dilepis*, gender can often be determined by examining the base of the tail immediately behind the cloaca. If the specimen is a male, bilateral swellings caused by the hemipenis (copulatory organ) may often be seen. In specimens of *Chamaeleo dilepis* as well as others related to it (*Chamaeleo calyptratus, Chamaeleo monachus*), tarsal spurs on the heels of the rear feet are found in young males.

Characteristics of Typical Chameleons

Typical chameleon adults have the remarkable ability to change color, and sexual dimorphism or dichromatism (in the case of *F. lateralis* and *F. campani*) exists in all the Malagasy species, and also in most African species. (*Chamaeleo melleri* is one of the rare exceptions where sexing the individual requires real expertise.)

Most typical chameleons are egg layers (oviparous), but a few species from East Africa are live bearers (ovoviviparous) and give birth to live babies (*Chamaeleo fuelleborni, Chamaeleo jacksonii, Chamaeleo hoehnelii, Chamaeleo werneri*).

Genus *Chamaeleo*

Typical chameleons have the greatest range of all chameleons, and live in various biomes and biotopes. The genus *Chamaeleo* is found all over Africa, in all types of environments (coastal deserts, savannas, grasslands, and forests). The common chameleon, *Cham-*

aeleo chamaeleo chameleon, has also been introduced in the temperate regions of southern Spain, Portugal, Sardinia, Sicily, and the Greek island of Crete, but its populations are dwindling and not believed to be solidly established. Other species of the genus *Chamaeleo* are present in the Middle East, down to the southern tip of the Indian subcontinent (*Chamaeleo zeylanicus*). *Chamaeleo's* subgenus, *Trioceros*, encompasses African horned chameleons, which are generally restricted to degraded or primary tropical and equatorial forests and afromontane forests of Western, Central, and Eastern Africa. In 1971, Jackson's chameleons (*Chamaeleo (Trioceros) jacksonii xantholophus*) were inadvertently introduced on Oahu, Hawaii, and today are considered established throughout most of the Hawaiian islands.

Artificial introduction of chameleons by humans is not something new. A viable population of *Chamaeleo africanus*, for example, exists in a regional pouch in Greece, from specimens that were apparently introduced from Africa by Roman soldiers. A green morph, though atypical population of Panther chameleons (*Furcifer pardalis*), which differs from the original species by the number of scales on its back, can be found in a small patch of vegetation in the outskirts of Saint Paul on La Réunion Island; it was probably introduced there several hundred years ago by seafarers. More recently, Veiled chameleons (*Chamaeleo calyptratus*) were

Furcifer rhinoceratus *(male)*.

released into the fragile Hawaiian ecosystem, where this species has now established itself.

Genus *Kinyongia*
Together with the genus *Chamaeleo*, the genus *Kinyongia* populates the mountainous, dense forests

Kinyongia fischeri multituberculata *(female).*

of tropical and equatorial East Africa. It comprises medium-sized and small chameleons with soft rostrums (*Kinyongia oxyrhina, K. tenuis*), the *fischeri* chameleon group (*K. excubitor, K. fisheri, K. tevetana, K. uthmoellerii*), the chameleons with single, flat, hard, protruding nasal appendices (*K. carpenteri, K. xenorhina*), and *K. adolfifriderici*. The similarities between the East African chameleons and some of the Malagasy species are striking; many aspects of their morphology and behavior resemble the genera *Furcifer* and a few species of *Calumma*, which are endemic to the Mascarene Islands.

Genus *Furcifer*

Chameleons of the genus *Furcifer* are essentially adaptable, nervous, sun-loving chameleons. They experience more rapid growth in their youth than chameleons of the genus *Calumma*, which are mainly restricted to the shade of tropical rainforests. *Furcifer* species are therefore more widespread over Madagascar and onto the other islands. Except for *Furcifer campani*, which lives at high altitude on the

Furcifer campani *is the sole Furcifer species found in altitude.*

sun-bathed grasslands of the Andringitra Massif Center East of Madagascar, they are found in various environments, from sea-level mangrove forests (*F. pardalis*) to mid-elevation forests (*F. balteatus, F. petteri*), coastal deciduous forests (*F. antimena, F. labordi*), tropical rainforests (*F. bifidus*), plateau forests (*F. minor*), and grass plateaus (*F. lateralis, F. oustaleti*).

Genus *Calumma*

Calumma species are primarily forest dwellers at low altitudes, but they also form the main group of species found at high altitude. From *C. tigris* in the Seychelles to *C. oshaughnessyi* in southeast Madagascar, where given the right cool and damp conditions, they can successfully adapt to various environments.

A male Calumma malthe *extends his neck flaps (occipital lobes) to woo a female.*

Availability

Several of the aforementioned typical chameleon species are available from pet shops, breeders, and wholesalers.

Characteristics of South African Dwarf Chameleons

South African dwarf chameleons are a genus of small chameleons about 6 inches (15 cm) long, either vividly colored (*Bradypodion pumilum*) or very dull (*B. gutturale*). All South African dwarves are ovoviviparous and give birth to a dozen live young usually once per year (rarely twice) during summertime. They can withstand cool to cold winters. They differ from true chameleons by a number of physiological aspects, such as broader jaws, gular projections, and a unique heterogeneous, bead-like scalation on their pink skin.

Range and Habitat

Bradypodion species are endemic to various biomes of the Republic of South Africa. These biomes include the fynbos areas (heartland); the coastal evergreen shrubland of the Cape Province; the arid plateaus of the Karoo region, with its low-lying succulent shrubs; and both temperate and subtropical mountain forests. In general, South African dwarves are found in microclimates with increased local humidity, such as the banks of rivers, the seashore, and gardens with sprinklers. Although some might survive in urban areas, certain dwarf species are threatened with habitat destruction by agriculture and land development; luckily, programs exist to incorporate the needs of human development and the survival of the concerned species.

Availability

South African dwarves are rarely available to the general public, as for the time being they cannot be legally exported for commercial purposes from South Africa.

Bradypodion damaranum *(male)*.

Characteristics of Stump-tailed Chameleons

All stump-tailed chameleons share a link to a common Brookesinae ancestor. The largest stump-tailed chameleon, *Brookesia perarmata*, which lives on Madagascar's no-less-impressive Bemahara karstic limestone massif, reaches a total length of 4 inches (11 cm). The smallest known species to date is *Brookesia minima*, at a bit over 0.6 inches (1.5 cm) long.

All stump-tailed chameleons are egg-laying species (not live bearers) characterized by their typical subdued colors, slow movements, and their failure to respond aggressively when seized. Besides these differences with their chameleon cousins, they have weakly prehensile or non-prehensile tails and depend more on their claws for climbing.

Morphology and Range

Stump-tailed chameleons of the genus *Brookesia* (except *Brookesia nasus*) have a tubular body ornamented with complex scalation that features dorsolateral projections, spinous bony scales, and supraorbital projections that might be regarded as passive means of defense against predators. *Rhampholeon* (African pygmy leaf chameleons) have longer tails (over 30 percent of the total length in males), rostral projections, and a leaf-like body similar to that of the typical

Brookesia peramata.

chameleons, to which they are more closely related. Most species are nestled in relics of wet mountain forests of eastern and southeastern Africa, with the exception of *Rhampholeon boulengeri*, a species widespread from the coastal forests of eastern Africa to the Ruwenzori Mountains of Uganda. *Rieppeleon* (East African

Rhampholeon acuminatus *(male)*.

11

Brookesia vadoni *(male). A chameleon found by Andre Peyrieras in 1968.*

pygmy chameleons) have short tails and no rostral projections. They are known by three species: *Rieppeleon brachyurus*, *R. brevicaudatus,* and *R. kerstenii*, a species that seem to adapt well to degraded environments.

Habitat and Egg Laying

All stump-tailed chameleons are inhabitants of primary forests (either deciduous or evergreen), and rely on the humidity of their surroundings (soil and air) for proper egg incubation and hatching of young. Indeed, female stump-tailed chameleons do not dig into the ground to lay their eggs. Instead, they leave them to hatch either on the forest floor or glued in a gecko-like manner under some kind of natural protection (*Br. perarmata*). For this reason, species found in deciduous primary forests might only lay their eggs at the onset of the wet season, which lasts for five to seven months. When the relative humidity of the atmosphere does not go lower than 75 percent, the humidity brings the forests back to life and stump-tailed chameleons out of their torpor. The rains allow for an abundant supply of insects, water, and milder temperatures. The stump-tailed chameleons' eggs usually hatch within a couple of months of being laid to benefit from the favorable conditions needed for their growth before slumping into dormancy during the dryer months.

Availability

Stump-tailed chameleons are usually available to the pet trade through importation of wild-caught specimens. Captive-bred specimens of *Rhampholeon brevicaudatus* are sometimes available as well.

Rieppeleon brachyurus *(male).*

Chapter Two

Elements of Chameleon Ecology

Habitats

Chamaeleonids use a variety of habitats including lowland and montane (Afro-alpine) primary forests, early and mature secondary forests, areas of cultivation (such as coffee plantations) surrounded by primary and secondary forests, actively logged forests, areas of dense human habitation (including cities), agricultural areas, grasslands, savannas, deserts, plateaus, coastal rainforests, and mangrove forests (*F. pardalis*). However, chameleons are bound by two critical elements: solar energy and relative humidity.

Solar Energy

First, they are tropical animals that rely primarily on solar radiation to keep their bodies at an optimal temperature. Chamaeleonids experience heat exchange passively and actively in four ways.

By conduction: A thermal exchange between the lizard and a surface. For example, when a Namaqua chameleon (*C. namaquensis*) in the desert gets overheated from standing on the ground, it buries itself deep into the sand—not just to escape the heat, but also to enjoy the cooling effect of the sand deeper below.

By convection: The movement of a gas or a liquid as it gets hotter (hot air rises as it warms, drawing cooler air in). Chameleons are sensitive enough to roost on perches that best correspond to their temperature preferences. For instance, the fins on the backs of some Cameroon chameleons increase the blood capillary surface and may allow the animals to slightly thermoregulate by dissipating or gaining heat from exposure to radiation.

By evaporation: When water molecules are evaporated by heat, they use caloric energy. As an example, seashores and undergrowth tropical forests offer milder temperatures and higher humidity because of the effect of water evaporation. Chameleons that are pale and panting are evaporating water through their airways and mouth to cool down.

By radiation: In cool atmospheres at altitude or in the morning, chameleons can be seen basking in

Furcifer lateralis *(male).*

the sun. They are absorbing solar (infrared) radiation to warm themselves and attain their optimal body temperature. In doing so, they also expose themselves to UV radiation; UVB is responsible for the photosynthesis of vitamin D, and UVA is responsible for regulating their circadian biorhythms through the parietal eye and for the release of various neuro-hormones produced by the hypothalamus. These hormones are responsible for several biological functions in the animals.

Relative Humidity

Second, chameleons are much more dependent on water than many other lizards. Even chameleon species living in xeric (hot and dry) areas such as the Namib Desert (*Chamaeleo namaquensis*) or the Sahara (*Chamaeleo c. chamaeleon*) can only be found along the marine coast of the desert or, in some oases for the latter. Under favorable conditions, a nighttime drop in temperature can lead to the formation of dew, a fairly regular occurrence in both the marine coast of deserts and mountain regions. This permits both plants and animals to obtain water in otherwise arid zones.

The relative humidity (RH) of the atmosphere is expressed in percentages (called hydrometric degrees). The RH is low when the air is dry; it is high when the atmosphere is saturated with water (after the rain in a rainforest, for example). Atmospheric humidity fluctuates with the seasons, and it also varies greatly depending on factors such as the terrain, the presence of water, mountains, forests, natural barriers to the wind, etc. Most chameleons do not fare well with an RH lower than 65 percent, and most species prefer an RH of 65 percent to 80 percent.

Many chameleons are so bound to a high-relative-humidity environment that they are only found in regions with microclimates with high rainfall. Over 60 percent of chameleon species live, in fact, in ever-moist forests, and very often along streams or small rivers. Other species have adapted to drier climates and tend to be more widespread outside of rainforests. Such is the case in Madagascar of the Oustalet's chameleon, (*Furcifer oustaleti*) and the Carpet chameleon (*F. lateralis*), two of the most widespread species of chameleons on

the island. Other species are literally born with the rains and disappear as the rainy season ends.

The most striking examples are probably *Furcifer labordi* and *Furcifer antimena* from the west coast of Madagascar. The region is xeric for seven months of the year and then becomes hot and humid for five months. Every year, new generations of chameleons are born in November, at the onset of the rainy season, from clutches deposited seven to eight months earlier, at the end of the annual rainy season. Along with the rains, the small patches of littoral (shoreline) spiny forests where they can be found come back to life and offer foliage to protect the chameleons from the harsh rays of the sun, provide plenty

Chamaeleo namaquensis, *a species restricted to the Namib desert of South Africa.*

An equatorial rainforest.

of food insects, and the right humidity and temperature to ensure that the babies, like all chameleons of the *Furcifer* group, experience a fast growth to adulthood (three months in their case). By the end of January, they are sexually mature, by March and April they lay some clutches of a few eggs, and soon afterward, the females start to die off en masse as the RH and temperature decrease.

Having bred both species in captivity, I observed animals rapidly going downhill when the RH was lower than 75 percent for a few days. Although laying eggs can take a great toll on the health of the females, it is possible that the animals are so dependent on precise humidity levels in their environment that they would die of the stress associated with a too-low humidity. Males of both species, though, have

been found living in the ground in the wintertime, and may survive the drier period buried in the ground to live another year. This might explain the great size differences observed in the males of these two species, while females are usually of the same size.

Population Dynamics

Wild chameleon populations in their habitats are either expanding, stable, or diminishing. Within a year, great fluctuations can be observed in the natural environments of several species (see previous paragraph), fluctuations that correlate with seasonal change. Depending on their normal life spans, whether the babies have just been born, if the adults are parading for reproduction, or if unfavorable weather has forced them into hiding, an area

might seem void of chameleons or densely populated.

While some chameleon populations boom and crash soon after the clutches of eggs have been laid (*F. antimena, F. labordi*, as previously noted), other populations (*C. gastrotaenia, C. nasuta*) that inhabit more stable habitats, can become very active at the onset of the cooler period of the year, when the babies are being born.

Equatorial species live in more stable climates, and their population censuses might seem to be more even year round. However, for species that strongly depend on their forests for a living, any large disruption, like the burning or slashing down of forests, would drastically affect their numbers.

Some localized species might be able to survive occasional tragic events (like the eruption of toxic volcanic gases from lakes around their forests, as has happened in Cameroon) with the hatchings emerging from clutches laid before the event and repopulating the forests. This shows their extraordinary resilience to even spectacular events that would normally wipe out all sorts of life forms for miles around.

In developing countries of Africa, chameleons' natural habitats are often threatened by human intervention, namely by agriculture and land development. Such is the case for some of the South African dwarves, who have been victimized by the use of pesticides, mechanical agriculture in the vineyards, and the construction of human habitats and roads.

Environment and Species Dispersal

Species living in relative geographic isolation, such as on small islands or on mountain peaks are at

A forest in northeastern Madagascar.

Furcifer antimena *females only live long enough to reproduce.*

the greatest risk of possible harm, because they depend on very small pockets of habitat for survival. Several million years ago, when the forest cover in Africa and Madagascar was in better shape than it is nowadays, chameleons knew more dependable climates and could move from one location to populate another with greater ease.

When climatic changes altered their environments, chameleons could either adapt through the evolutionary process, or they could migrate in search of another, more favorable habitat. When they could neither migrate nor adapt, they died. Thus, as the climates became untenably dry, hot, or cool on the plains or the mountains of Africa and Madagascar, the chameleon species found there adapted or dispersed as

they could, either by chance or by necessity. Some dispersals probably occurred when trees fell during storms and were carried away by the gush of a river flow or oceanic current. Dispersions were either radial (the ecological factors encouraged movements in all directions around the original site), or linear (the ecological conditions encouraged movement in one direction only).

Those that dispersed colonized other hospitable areas and diversified, first to variations, then with time and the accumulation of the retained genetic mutations—sometimes changes just slightly affected adult size, cranial adornments, or idiosyncrasies—to subspecies, and finally to full species, resulting in all the chameleon species that have ever existed.

Habitats and Biotopes

Different species of chameleons often share the same habitat (sympatric species), but rarely do they inhabit the same biotope. As we have seen, chameleons are mostly arboreal lizards, and in forests several biotopes exist and several species might coexist. Some species have adapted to living on or near the ground, such as stump-tailed chameleons. In Equatorial Africa, the Crested chameleon (*Chamaeleo cristatus*) never gets farther than six feet off the ground in an ever-cool, humid, and shady environment. The tree canopy of the same forests, at the tops of the highest trees, is also an ecosystem in itself, quite different from the one below. It is sunny, hot, and humid, and some species rarely descend from it except to deposit their clutches, like the Owen's chameleon (*Chamaeleo oweni*). Often, one may spot differences in the morphologies of these species, probably linked to their habitats. For example, *Chamaeleo cristatus*, which lives near the ground, has a shorter tail than the flighty species that might let themselves fall from trees to escape their predators, using their long, whipping tails to catch a branch before hitting the ground.

When species that are closely related live in the same habitat and their populations overlap, they may breed and create hybrids. As a matter of fact, hybrids are likely a common occurrence in some *Furcifer* species from Madagascar, where

A hybrid of Furcifer pardalis *and* Furcifer oustaleti *(male).*

several *Furcifer* species overlap. Several species of male chameleons in the genus *Furcifer* live in environments that are only seasonally adequate for their reproduction. These chameleons do not engage in lengthy courtship, and they are sexually aroused by the stimulus signal of a uniform coloration (green or brown) on any other chameleon in sight, which might be mistaken for a female of their own species. When a male of one species gets turned on by the coloration of a female of another species, hybridization of these two species might occur. Because these species are sympatric (they share the same environment) and because they are related to a certain extent, viable babies could be born from a deposited clutch. I have been thinking for some

*The Angel's chameleon (*Furcifer angeli*) lives in a region where populations of* F. rhinoceratus *and* F. pardalis *interlap and might be a hybrid of the two species.*

Chameleons: Camouflage Experts or Showy Artists?

In the general public's mind, chameleons select and change their coloration to resemble their surroundings. Some may go as far as stating that the surface on which they sit dictates the lizards' color and pattern choice, just as in octopuses or squids.

Chameleons are indeed, just like us, extremely visual animals. This is one thing besides opposable toes we have in common with them (and may explain the kind of "special connection" we often feel with them). It is in the interest of chameleons to avoid their most common predators: birds and snakes. Birds, just like chameleons, have excellent vision, and also like chameleons, they happen to perceive light in the UV range, seeing colors that we cannot imagine; birds of prey even see in the infrared range. That is to say, they may have a richer experience in seeing the world than we do. Snakes, on the other hand, mostly rely on their sense of smell, heat sensors and vibration detection to prey on their victims.

So, the more conspicuous the chameleon is to predators, the more trouble it might find itself in. The methods of camouflage used by chameleons involve cryptic body shape and coloration as well as locomotion (or lack of movement,

time of *F. angeli* as a possible hybrid of *F. pardalis* and *F. rhinoceratus*, *F. belalandaensis* as the offspring of *F. antimena* and *F. lateralis*, and *F. tuzetae* as a crossing of *F. antimena* and *F. verrucosus*. Hybrids are probably a rather frequent occurrence within related species of chameleons of the genus *Furcifer*, because they are more prone to be sexually aggressive than the other genera and usually do not engage in lengthy courtships.

Furcifer tuzetae *(male)*.

called akynesis in stump-tailed chameleons). For example, tree-dwelling species are more active when the wind blows; their faltering gaits then resemble the movement of windblown leaves, and their vertically flattened bodies enhance this impression.

Camouflage is very important for a creature that does not move very quickly, yet is a predator. "Seeing without being seen" is a special and important adaptation. A recent study seems to have demonstrated that in the South African species *Bradypodion taeniabronchum*, color change is in fact a means to blend in. The chameleons reacted to the presence of a bird of prey by darkening their skin, possibly so as to match the branch on which they stood. When faced with a snake, they would turn a lighter color, possibly to be less

conspicuous against the sky background.

If most of the stump-tailed chameleons are rather drab in coloration, some species like *Brookesia vadoni* and several species of *Rhampholeon* show some pigmentation both to camouflage themselves but also to facilitate communication between the animals. Young chameleons are usually brown or green in coloration until they reach adulthood. Then, under the influence of hormonal change, their true colors begin to show.

The actual coloration of the true chameleons varies depending on a combination of internal and external cues. Among the former are species, gender, age, emotional state, and physical health of the lizard. Among the external factors, temperature and light intensity predominate. The

Juvenile **Furcifer minor** *(female).*

emotional state of the animal is affected by many things, not the least important being the presence of other chameleons (of either sex) of the same species.

Chameleons that have the greatest ability for color change use their flashiest colors to get noticed by other chameleons. Flashy colors are used by males to either woo females and gain their acceptance as mates, or to scare male competitors away from their surroundings. Chameleons, in fact, use conspicuous colors and body positioning as a means to communicate with one another, to signal their presence and their status to others.

True chameleons have skins that are in some parts strongly UV reflective, and like many other lizards, they perceive light in the UV range. Thanks to this ability and to the fact that leaves of trees generally absorb UV radiation, they might, in the wild, be able to spot fellow chameleons from several meters away, while staying largely undetectable to other animals. Visual signals might be used in various encounters with individuals of different species or sexes for the purpose of reproduction or defense of the territory. I also think that chameleons, just like some other animals, might be able to see polarized light and that some parts

Most chameleon behaviors are genetically programmed. Calumma furcifer *(male) in a threat display.*

of their skins actually scatter and decompose the light with various polarities. These selectively reflective skin markings can be observed on the shoulders of males of *Calumma furcifer*, a species living sympatrically with *Calumma gastrotaenia*. The females of both species are very similar, and the males' markings might help the species in mate signalization. Without the ability to perceive polarized light and the reflection on the skin of the males, females of both species might copulate with the wrong mate.

Male chameleons advertise their presence to one another by a display of colors, some of which are not perceived by us. When two males meet, a joust usually ensues. The winner will show his brightest colors, whereas the submissive chameleon will darken his coloration (its dark skin makes it less conspicuous to

the other chameleon's eyes). At times, a very scared chameleon (one that has just escaped from death or a terrible predator, for example) will appear very dark and prostrated, but if the animal feels it has been wronged, and is bold enough, it might show some aggression along with its darkened skin coloration.

Furcifer minor *mating. Adults advertise to each other by showing bright colors.*

Chapter Three
Elements of Chameleon Biology

Origins

All chameleon species that have ever existed branched out around 45 million years ago (give or take 15 million years) from one common ancestor, probably a lizard like *Calotes,* an agamid lizard that shares common genetic material with chameleons and also shows vivid coloration change, independently moving eyes, and the ability to climb trees. Approximately ten million years later, it is thought that chamaeleonids branched further from a basal ancestor of Brookesinae (the Madagascan stump-tailed chameleons) into the genera *Bradypodion, Calumma, Chamaeleo, Furcifer, Kinyongia, Nadzikambia, Rhampholeon*, and *Rieppeleon*. Under environmental pressure from changing climates and desertification, these groups split up over the years into other species and took refuge higher in the mountains.

It seems that, on several occasions, radial dispersions of chameleons took place out of Madagascar— probably by logs or tree rafts carried on ocean currents—to populate Africa, the Seychelles, and the Mascarene Islands. The relocated chameleons later diverged into new species. If this theory is proven correct, it would make Madagascar the birthplace of many species of chameleons existing today. We do know that chameleons are an old group of lizards that was once widely distributed, as evidenced by fossils found in Bavaria, Mongolia, China, and Kenya. The oldest chameleon fossil was found in Central Europe, in Bohemia, and has been dated at around 26 million years (Miocene period) and named *Chamaeleo caroliquarti*.

Physiology

Activity

Chamaeleonids are diurnal, poikilotherm animals, and their physical activities are affected by the cycles of day and night and of the seasons. In rare cases, a chameleon might be found wandering on the ground at night (probably because it fell from its branch), and some females might still be busy in their nests with oviposition, but chameleons usually stop all activity in the dark. They also fall into slumber with decreasing temperatures.

Thermoregulation

Poikilotherms have no internal body-temperature regulating mechanisms. When their bodies cool below a certain internal temperature, hypothermia occurs and enzymatic activity is also reduced. Conversely, when overheated, hyperthermia quickly results in cell damage, and enzymatic reactions are also impeded. Either condition can prove fatal, but the latter one is quicker. Thus, the metabolic functions and the very life of any poikilotherm depend on its ability to maintain a suitable body temperature by utilizing external thermal energy.

In their environments, chamaeleonids do not always encounter ideal temperatures. Some days can be very cold, while others may be hot and dry. Thus it is necessary for chameleons, like other lizards, to use their morphological characteristics to help regulate their body temperature.

A cold chameleon can increase its body temperature by several degrees by positioning itself in the sunlight, darkening its color, and modifying the volume of air contained in its lungs. Conversely, a warm chameleon may reduce its body temperature by moving into the shade, lightening its body color, and panting. Not only does this

Furcifer willsii *(male) basking to increase his body temperature.*

reduce heat absorption, but moisture evaporation from the mucous membranes of the mouth, throat, primary digestive tract, and respiratory tract can actually cool the lizard. In these ways, chamaeleonids are able to maintain their body temperatures within the necessary parameters, and often may actually attain the optimum temperature needed for their functioning: preferred body temperature, or PBT. PBT varies per

Chamaeleo (trioceros) pfefferi *(male) with opposable toes.*

species, specimen, age, gender, and level of activity, but for chameleons it usually ranges between 72.8 and 82°F (23 to 28°C).

Anatomy

Toes

The toes on chameleons' feet are separated into groups of twos and threes: three fused toes on the outside of the rear feet and the inside of the front feet, and two toes on the outside of the front feet and the inside of the hind feet. Most chamaeleonids have simple claws, but those of the genus *Rhampholeon* have bicuspid claws. The inner soles of the feet are endowed with many nerve endings,

allowing the lizards to sense surfaces, and conical pads that secure their grip, allowing them to walk without really watching where they are putting their feet.

Head

Chameleons' heads are shaped, to accommodate for their bulging eyes, in either a triangle or a lozenge shape. The heads of the Brookesinae lack the nasal appendices found on the Rhampholeoninae (pygmy leaf chameleons), but both groups include species with preorbital projections *(B. vadoni, R. acuminatus)*.

Chameleon jaws are equipped with a set of rudimentary, identical teeth, which are an extension of the bone (no socket like in mammals);

this type of dentition is known as acrodont. Teeth are there to seize, not to masticate, so their prey is pretty much ingested whole.

Body

What is striking in typical chameleons and some stump-tailed chameleons are their vertically flattened bodies. Some Brookesinae and at least *Rhampholeon kerstenii* show some rather tubular-shaped bodies, more like the bodies of lizards.

Tail

The tail of chamaeleonids can be very short (as in some *Rhampholeon*), or exceptionally long and prehensile (as in other species like *F. balteatus*). It is frequently adorned with spines and osseous (bony) projections in stump-tailed chameleons. Sailfin-like ornaments on the tail are solely found in the Cameroon crested chameleon group.

The tail is used as a balancing pole during a walk, as a fifth limb while climbing, when securing a grip for the hands to reach another branch, as a hook in case of a fall, and as part of the threat display when it is coiled to appear larger or displayed as a potential whip to intimidate a rival. Unlike those of many other lizards, chameleons' tails are not regenerative, but many chameleons survive amputated tails.

Many chameleons coil their tails as a threat display to appear larger.

Sensory Organs

Eyes: Chamaeleonids rely heavily on their sophisticated eyes for survival. As in many species of vertebrates (fishes, lizards, and birds), their eyes have the ability to move independently. But chamaeleons' eyes can rotate by 180 degrees in almost every direction on each side of the head, independently of each other. Their eyes are mostly covered with scaled skin, and offer a narrow

Eye of Calumma parsonii *(male).*

line lenses, which are akin to having a telephoto lens. Their retinas are equally elaborate, with a very large number of rods, and are sensitive to daylight and UVA rays (300 to 400 nanometers). The optical nerves are the largest ones in their bodies, and they are endowed with enlarged optical lobes in their brains.

Although their eyes are very well protected—chamaeleonids have a shut-eye reflex when they are attacking prey, and the pupils retract behind a special bone during their sleep—elements can lodge between the eyelid and the eyeball and cause discomfort to the animals. To clean their eyes, chameleons make use of their eye muscles to push out their eyeballs and rub their eyelids against branches.

Chameleons have eye-brain reflexes in response to fast movements, shiny surfaces, and colors. Anything smaller than a chameleon moving fast and shining, or presenting an attractive coloration they interpret as prey. Anything larger and moving fast they interpret as a potential predator or aggressor.

Parietal Eye: Chamaeleonids, like many other reptiles, are endowed with a most fascinating organ: the parietal eye. The parietal eye is best known in the New Zealand sphenodontids, such as the tuatara, and is often called the "third eye." It is indeed a vestigial eye, found in many

field of vision through a small opening in the eyelids, but they can see fine details from far away. Chameleons rely on their binocular vision to judge distances so as to catch their prey, and their eyes are thus equipped with a remarkable set of lenses: the cornea and the crystal-

Furcifer bifidus *(female). The parietal eye, which is quite small in chameleons, is covered by scales and not externally visible.*

Chameleons are attracted to shiny things, and they recognize eyes. Interestingly, their eyelids, which are adorned with markings or flashy colors, are very often noticeable from far away.

Calumma parsonii *(male) aiming at its prey.*

lizards between the other two eyes and sometimes covered with scales, sometimes (in iguanids) not. This organ is light-sensitive, but it reacts only to specific wavelengths—those responsible, in part, for sensation of the blue and violet colors, and UVA. This organ is linked by a nerve to the pineal gland, a section of the hypothalamus responsible for regulating many of the chamaeleonids' hormonal functions. Depending on the time of year (or the position of the earth toward the sun, for species sensitive to climatic variations), more UVA rays pass through the earth's atmosphere and, in turn, the parietal eye gets more or less stimulation, with more or less effect on the limbic system of the brain.

Tongue: If the sense of smell is rudimentary in chamaeleonoids— possibly thanks to the Jacobson's organ, which is responsible for the sense of smell in reptiles and visible on the mouth palate—their sense of taste is rather refined. Taste buds have been found on their tongues, and as anyone who has kept chameleons knows, they have definite meal preferences, seeming to go for one prey rather than another when given the choice. From a young age, the babies learn to differ-

entiate between edible and unpalatable prey, but some of this knowledge is innate.

Chamaeleonids capture their prey by shooting their tongues at it. The tip of the tongue becomes enlarged and acts as a suction pad as soon as it contacts its prey; it is then immediately retracted into the mouth. Chameleons' tongues can be surprisingly long and extend well over the body size (snout to vent, SV) of the animal. For an explanation of the tongue-shooting mechanism, see page 34.

Skin

The chameleon's skin is mostly made of proteins (keratin) and lipids (fats). Scales vary from species to species and cover most of the body and appendages. It may be homogeneous (*Chamaeleo deremensis*), heterogeneous (*Bradypodion* spp.), bead-like (*Chamaeleo chamaeleon*),

Shedding Precaution

Should a chameleon have an incomplete shedding, the remaining patches of skin are likely to allow for bacterial growth between the leftover skin and the epidermis; permanent damage to the chameleon's skin may ensue.

rough (several species of stump-tailed chameleons), or velvety (*Furcifer willsii*). The primary function of chameleons' skin is to ensure the preservation of body integrity. It is a barrier to protect the internal organs and works to keep an appropriate homeostasis (proper internal chemical balance and body temperature). It is also used as a cloak for stealth and an organ to communicate. The chromatophores (cells responsible for the change of skin color) are sensitive and reactive to infrared, UV, and some part of the visible light spectrum, but the protective role of the integument (the external part of the Chamaeleonids' skins) is limited to inner water retention and thermoregulation, as they do not possess sebaceous glands which provide sebum (a chemical compound with a low pH bacteria and is a water repellant).

Chamaeleonids do not shed their skins in one piece, but rather exfoliate in patches. Shedding occurs more frequently in times of rapid growth and less frequently when growth is slow or the animal is ill. In a shedding chameleon, the epidermis cracks along the borders between the scales or squama, then separates from the newly formed skin beneath. The old pieces of skin dry up and harden, then flake off. The shedding process can take a few days, but it is necessary that it be completed. When sections of skin fail to shed, chameleons attempt to rub them off on branches, and since flaking skin on the eyelids and snout may impair vision, chameleons try to remove them as quickly as possible. Chameleons are

A color variation in a male **Chamaeleo montium.**

A shedding F. antimena.

naturally attracted to shed skins, and they will often eat their own or another chameleon's shed.

Nerve sensors are found in the skin of chameleons. Other than photo receptivity (light and heat), their skin surfaces are particularly sensitive to pressure (touch).

Internal ear: Chamaeleonids' ears have simplified over time, and they are not visible externally, being covered with skin and scales. Unlike other lizards, chamaeleonids possess neither an exterior aperture nor a tympanic membrane, but they share some skeletal and fluid structure similarities with snakes. These structures on the sides of their skulls and at the back of their eye sockets may be effective at picking up bass waves. Chameleons are known to pick up a narrow range of sound vibrations, from 200 Hz to 600 Hz, depending on species, and lowland species seem to have a wider range of sensitivity. Chamaeleonids are

also known to emit purrs from their bodies, much like the way alligators emit infrasonic vibrations. These extremely low vibrations are fairly common in the animal kingdom, from fishes to giraffes and elephants, and are able to travel over long distances and through a lot of obstacles, such as through the forests and savannas. These purrs can be felt to the touch and may be a means of communication with other chameleons.

Highland chameleons such as this Chamaeleo hoehnelii *male have lower hearing capacities than lowland chameleon species.*

Chapter Four

Chameleon Biology and Physiology

Hunting

True chameleons are carnivorous insectivores that hunt for their food. Food provides the animals with the energy they need for all their metabolic functions (behavior, growth, reproduction). Analyses of their stomach contents and fresh droppings, as well as on-the-spot observations, disclose that—besides insects—vertebrates (lizards, frogs, birds, and small mammals), snails, other invertebrates (spiders, centipedes), and plant materials (fresh and dead leaves, bark) are also intentionally consumed by chameleons on occasion. Stump-tailed chameleons, however, are not active foragers preying on small invertebrates; instead, they employ the "sit-and-wait" strategy.

Sometimes, one type of food source makes up the bulk of what chamaeleonids feed on in their habitats; tenebrionid beetles are the main staple for *Chamaeleo namaquensis*, spiders comprise up to 75 percent of the diet in *Calumma cucullata*, flies are the staple food for *C. jacksonii,* and locusts sustain *Chamaeleo chamaeleon.* Usually unable to tear their prey apart, chameleons ingest it whole; the largest chameleons are known to feed occasionally on small mammals, birds, and frogs. Even though invertebrates form the overwhelming bulk of the diet in all species, some chameleons have been observed tongue-darting at fishes in the water or seizing small eggs with their jaws.

Chameleons capture mobile prey by shooting their tongues from a distance at them. They also use their jaws to bite at snails, eggs, and plant materials, like other lizards do.

Biological Functions

Digestive and Urinary Systems

Chamaeleonids have a rather simple digestive system. Once the food is seized between the jaws, it is crushed with their small, triangular teeth, chewed, and pushed with the help of the tongue from the mouth down to the esophagus and into the stomach, which is essentially tubular. There, strong acids and extremely active enzymes initiate a chemical reaction to start breaking down the ingested materials. The absorption of molecules and nutrients occurs in the intestinal tract, which is rather short, and the wastes are excreted through the cloaca. The liver and the pancreas are annexed to the digestive system and help in the process.

The urinary passages are distinct from the generative canals, although both lead to the cloaca. The feces and urine, excreted together as droppings, consist largely of urate solids suspended in a transparent, jelly-like fluid.

Respiratory and Cardio-circulatory Systems

Chameleons are air-breathing creatures. Gas exchange occurs through respiration, in the alveoli (small blood vessel-lined sacs where oxygen is taken in by the blood cells and carbon dioxide given off) of the lungs. The lungs in chamaeleonids are either simple (unilobed), as in Brookesinae, or subdivided in two lobes (bilobed), as in most chameleons. Lungs with relatively few alveoli are limited in the amount of oxygen transfer that can take place at a given time, and chameleon blood is relatively low in red blood cells. This might in part explain the slowness of chameleons. They also do not require oxygen to heat their bodies, and they rely on other sources of energy other than

Calumma cucullata *lives in the undergrowth of primary northeastern forests of Madagascar and mainly feeds on spiders.*

glycogen oxidation to provide for outbursts of physical activity.

Their blood is carried through a system of veins and arteries linking the various organs to the lungs and the heart. The heart is three chambered, with two atria supplying the single ventricle. In the heart, venous and arterial blood mix; this, again, limits the amount of oxygenated blood reaching the organs.

Immune System

Chameleons have to defend themselves against numerous

The Chameleon's Curious Tongue

The tongue-shooting mechanism has been studied numerous times by several researchers. The tongue is made up of a group of muscles standing on a bone in the middle of the throat, called the hyoid bone. The base and the column of the tongue consist of a collection of round muscles called sphincters, akin to a pile of discs. At its base, the tongue is held in place by a pair of muscles attached to the hyoid bone and the jaw. The apex (tip) of the tongue features an enlarged muscle, endowed with glands secreting sticky saliva and, when observed under a microscope, small hooks and rings on its surface that assist in the capture and retention of prey. When a chameleon spots its prey, both its eyes focus on it and evaluate the distance; then its tongue emerges and darts over to the prey. Upon hitting the prey, the tip of the tongue spreads over it, and as it is being pulled back into the mouth, a vacuum on the contact surface is created. When retracting its tongue into its mouth, the chameleon shuts its eyes for protection and crushes the prey with its jaws before swallowing it whole.

viruses, bacteria, parasites, and other pathogenic agents in their environment, air, prey, water, and elsewhere.

The first barrier against disease is a damage-free skin; however, chameleons' skins are not protected by acidic glandular secretions like in other animals, which limits their immune function. Other external barriers are the mucous membranes and their secretions (saliva, gastric acid). In addition to these, chameleons have an internal immune system in the blood in the form of white cells (lymphocytes, monocytes, plasmacytes, and antibodies), antimicrobial proteins (also found in the saliva), as well as other specific cells.

In order to stay fit, chameleons rely on adequate nutrition, rich in natural and complex antioxidants, an adequate environment, offering the right humidity and temperature, and light.

Homeostasis

Water is vital to chameleons. As with all animals, water is essential for the healthy functioning of chameleons' physiological systems, as their cells can only operate in a largely aqueous environment: their bodies. Chameleons take in water either by ingesting it from their environments by licking drops of water with their tongues (morning dew in the desert, rain in other places), or by inhaling it (coastal fog in the desert, mist or ambient humidity in wet areas).

Chameleons must replace the water they lose through the skin, and by breathing, excreting, and thermoregulation. Species living in humid environments are far more sensitive and prone to water loss if exposed to drier conditions than species adapted to arid habitats.

Metabolic organic waste in chameleons is expelled through the cloaca in a jelly-like substance as peanut-shaped feces (brown) and a quantity of uric acid crystals in a white-yellowish paste, which usually comes after the feces. Excreting uric acid as crystals allows chameleons to use little water (and thus save it for other metabolic functions), but it has two disadvantages: it is energy costly to produce, and if the chameleon's drinking water is scarce for too long, excretion of uric acid will be inhibited, causing gout. (see Chapter 12)

Endocrinal and Reproductive Systems

Chameleons, like all other vertebrates, rely on their endocrinal and neuronal glands (pituitary gland, hypothalamus) for the production of hormones. Released in the blood, these hormones ensure a proper chemical balance necessary for growth and sexual development, to regulate the physiological functions (osmoregulation, biorhythms like reproduction, sleep, food intake, etc.), and to prompt changes in behavior (courtship, female receptiveness or the opposite).

Hormones target specific cells in the body, in which they induce complex chemical reactions responsible

Calumma boettgeri (male).

for the modification or destruction of the targeted cells. Many of these hormones are controlled by the hypothalamus, a region of the brain that receives information from various organs, including the parietal eye.

Both male and female chameleons have paired gonads, situated near the kidneys. The females have two oviducts, which serve as a uterus. The males have two erectile hemipenes that are located in pouches at the ventral base of their tails, behind the cloaca.

Nervous System

Hormones and nerves are responsible for carrying information through the body and fostering communication between cells. In chameleons, the nervous system is well developed and comprises a brain (encephala), a spinal cord (dorsal neural tube), nerves, and nerve sensors. The brain has left and right hemispheres, which are quite distinct from each other, twelve pairs of cranial nerves, and a

Calumma gallus *(male).*

spinal cord with ganglions, from which the spinal nerves branch out to the rest of the body.

The Change of Colors Phenomenon

Many chamaeleonids, like some other animals (mollusks, fishes, and other lizards), have evolved highly specialized pigmented cells in their skins that are responsible for their spectacular display of colors. Physiologically speaking, the phenomenon is the result of two factors acting on the skin's specialized color cells, called chromatophores.

One factor is pure optical physics. Called the Tyndall effect, it is responsible for scattering light into particles that reflects only some particular wavelengths from sunlight and absorbs the others. The other factor is neuro-hormonal and depends on the chameleon's physical and psychological status.

Seen under a microscope, a chameleon's skin consists of an upper layer, the epidermis, and a lower layer, the dermis. The epidermis is made up of transparent, hardened cells, under which are cells that have not yet hardened (the Malpighian layer). The epidermis is the white skin the chameleons shed as it grows. The Malpighian layer contains guanocytes, which are skin

How Chameleons Change Color

Pigment	Coloring Effect	Cells
Guanine (protein)	Lightening: white	Guanocytes
Purines	Optical: Tyndall effect	Iridocytes
Carotenoids (lipids)	Yellow	Xanthophores
Melanin (protein)	Darkening: black, blue, violet	Melanophores
Carotenoids (lipids)	Red	Erythrocytes

cells that appear yellow against a light background and blue against a dark background. If we put a piece of chameleon skin on a glass slide illuminated from below, the skin appears yellow; if we shut off the microscope's light, the skin appears blue.

You can check this on Panther chameleons. Their horizontal bar turns either white or blue depending on their mood.

Between the dermis and the epidermis are refractive cells called iridocytes. These cells are also responsible for the Tyndall effect, as they diffuse only a part of the sunlight reaching them. Depending on the position of the iridocytes, the light might pass up through the transparent dead cells of the epidermis, or it might penetrate farther down into the skin mass to affect the other color cells: the contractile chromatophores.

The contractile chromatophores are cells containing fatty pigments

that have branches reaching to the dermis. When they are contracted, the colors show below the surface of the chamaeleonids' skins, but not when they are at rest (when they sleep, for example). There are three types of contractile chromatophores: the xanthophores, containing yellow pigment, the erythrophores (red pigment), and the melanophores (brown

Captive bred **Furcifer labordi** *(female) sleeping.*

or black pigment). You can check this on gravid Veiled chameleons. Their skins seem to be covered with colorful dots.

The contractile chromatophores are subject to neuro-hormonal influences. A hormone called intermedin acts on the large sympathetic nerve of the chamaeleonids, which then initiates the contraction or the relaxation of the chromatophores.

When a chameleon is at rest, the contractile chromatophores lie under the dermis and the iridocytes diffuse the light back through the guanocytes in the epidermis. The skin may appear pale yellow, green (yellow + blue), even white. If the chameleon is annoyed, the iridocytes move, light diffuses through the dermis, the erythrophores and melanophores contract, and the animal displays vivid warning colors. When the animal is active and unthreatened, the iridocytes move again, light is diffused through the dermis, the xanthophores contract to show beautiful colors, and the patterns become brighter as the melanophores rest.

Color plays its role in the thermoregulation of the animals. When a chameleon is cold and needs to increase its body temperature, its iridocytes allow more light to penetrate the skin, the skin colors darken under the contraction of the melanophores, and the animal flattens its body to provide greater surface area for light absorption. You can check this on basking chameleons.

The contractile chromatophores cells are found in three distinct layers, which successively show yellow, black or brown, and red deep into the dermis. The carotenoid pigments responsible for the yellow and the red colors are often joined to protein pigments, modifying colors even more.

Reproduction

Territoriality and Courtship

Male chameleons in breeding condition will advertise their status by displaying flashy coloration at all times while surveying their surroundings in search of a potential female partner. When interloping males find themselves in the presence of one another, they rapidly intensify their coloration, inflate their bodies and gular pouch, coil their tails, stand as high as they can on their feet, and start rocking on their branches. When the threat is not enough to discourage one opponent, they resort to threatening one another in a chicken game of flaring colors, rolling tails, gaping mouths, and, for species that have them, extended neck flaps. At times, when both opponents are confident of winning the contest, a fight will ensue; the animals will come face to face, trying to bite at each other. Species with horns will use them in their joust, until the opponent is pushed away, flees on his own, or positions himself underneath the branch with a dark, submissive coloration to indicate surrender. Non-gravid females and young animals

Courtship in C. parsonii *yellow giant morph.*

are usually passive and do not show much territorial instinct.

If a male spots a female sitting in his vicinity, he will display his brightest colors in the hope of getting her attention. When necessary, the male will leave his territory to join the female on her territory. He will make sure to get her attention through rocking head motions, performing little shimmies for her, and sometimes emitting what feel to the touch like brief purrs. If the female is receptive, she remains totally passive. When not in the mood, she will send some visual signals, such as opening her mouth and, rocking her body on a branch while keeping an eye on the suitor. It often happens that a female will use her forearm to reject a pushy male, and leave the branch she sat on, only to be pursued by the male, at times for days.

In sun-loving species, courtship is usually expedited or short, and nongravid females are left with little choice in the matter. In species living in the shade or in evergreen environments, courtship might last for days, with the males following the females (*C. parsonii*) or even being carried on the backs of their mates (*Brookesia minima*).

Copulation

When a male mounts a female, he starts by seizing the tail, and then the flanks, to position himself on the back of the female. During copulation, the male will contort his body and tail until the cloacae of the pair are aligned. The female usually lifts her tail, and the male's blood-engorged hemipenis is inserted into the female's cloaca. Actual copulation may last from several minutes to three hours. During this time, it is possible to witness a considerable darkening in some females' coloration as they undergo hormonal changes. Upon completion, the male withdraws the now flaccid hemipenis, and the-no-longer passive female moves away as quickly as she possibly can. At times, she might show some aggression toward her mate.

Fertilization

Nearly one fifth of all the true chameleons are ovoviviparous (livebearers) species; the other species are oviparous (egg-laying).

Both in oviparous and ovoviviparous species that experience seasonal climatic variations, breeding and hatching (birthing in the case of ovoviviparous) are contingent on favorable weather. Species living in

Sperm Storage

Several female chamaeleonids have seminal receptacles meant for active spermatozoa retention, allowing delayed fertilization and production of additional fertile clutches without the presence of males. It is possible that some females even store the sperm of different males, as some species are known to copulate with several males during their receptive period.

rather uniform climates year round may reproduce at any time.

At the favorable period, and if the female chameleons have had enough food to eat, they will start to ovulate; in other words, their bodies will start producing ovules from follicles in their ovaries. In every female, each follicle consists of an egg cell coated with multiple membranes. Ovulation means that the follicle membranes surrounding the ovules tear, and the ovules enter the abdominal cavity. In chameleons, fertilization is internal: during copulation, the male chameleon inserts one of its erect hemipenes in the female's cloaca, releasing his spermatozoids the female's reproductive system.

Once the ovules have been fertilized, they pass into the glandular portion of the oviduct, where they are coated with different secretions on their journey. In oviparous species, the embryo is surrounded by yolk, albumen, an egg mem-

Mating C. malthe.

Gravid female chameleons present specific coloration. Furcifer balteatus.

brane, and an eggshell. In addition, the eggs have embryonic extensions such as the amnion, allontois, and an umbilical vesicle, but unlike bird eggs, they do not contain the chalaza that suspends the yolk within the center of the albumen.

In ovoviviparous species, the eggs are kept in the female's body, and live birth usually occurs four to six months after impregnation. Species like *C. jacksonii* in the wild give birth a couple of times per year, in correlation with the start of the rainy seasons, first to a small clutch in June and then to a larger clutch in December.

In other species of chameleons, egg deposition happens one to six months after mating, depending on the species and, at times, the individual female.

Egg Laying (Oviposition)

Gravid oviparous females generally come to the ground to find a suitable nesting spot and start digging a burrow into the earth. As mentioned in Chapter 2, one species of chameleon in the Seychelles, *Calumma tigris*, makes use of the space between pineapple leaves to lay its eggs, whereas rainforest stump-tailed chameleons leave their eggs on the soil litter, and deciduous forest stump-tailed chameleons protect them from heat under pieces of wood.

Eggshells

The shells of chameleon eggs are flexible and leathery. They are very permeable to water and gas, and will gain in volume and weight during their incubation. One exception to this is the *Brookesia perarmata*, which lays sticky eggs that can adhere to any surface and whose shells harden within twenty minutes of their exposure to air.

Close up of chameleon eggs.

To egg-laying females, soil temperature (for proper egg development), the feel of the soil to the touch (for spacing out the eggs), moisture (needed to hatch the clutch), and plant cover (for the babies to disperse safely) are important considerations. They start digging after choosing their spot, most of the time in the morning. The work may span over a couple of days, and if they are disturbed, females will leave their chosen site to go lay their eggs somewhere else.

Female chameleons use all four feet in digging their nests. The burrow is usually shallow, although deeper nests have been observed where the substrate is particularly soft. Egg-laying chameleons prefer soils with a slight sandy feel to them.

When the hole is complete, the female backs into it and starts expulsing the eggs one by one. At times, the eggs can be connected to one another by a thin membrane, or they might be fused by a twin wall (*C. wiedersheimi*). When oviposition has taken place, the female fills the burrow as completely as possible, in what looks like an attempt to obliterate external signs of disturbance. The air inside the nesting chamber will ensure proper gas exchange among the aggregated eggs. The eggs' permeability to gases, water, and chemical components allows for a kind of sibling solidarity—for example, as water is passed from one egg to another in times of drought.

Clutches vary from two eggs (Brookesinae) to seventy eggs and more (*C. melleri, C. calyptratus*). The yolk is the source of nutrition and energy for the embryo, as it is naturally rich in calcium, carotenoids, vitamin D_3, vitamin E, and iodine; the embryo will tap into the egg yolk for its growth. Ovoviviparous species retain eggs without calcareous shells in the oviducts until the young are ready to be born. Thermoregulation by the females permits the correct development of the embryos. The eggs develop in the enlarged portion of the oviduct, which plays a role similar to that of the mammalian uterus.

With oviparous species, eggs are laid sometimes in more or less advanced embryonic form. The eggs may go through a dormant period (diapause) especially in species living in marked climatic conditions, making incubation times variable.

Development of the Embryos and Hatching

After the gravid females have laid their eggs, the eggs are left to themselves under the influence of natural elements to properly develop. This development can be, depending on species and weather, suspended temporarily. In Malagasy chameleons, many species will lay eggs at the end of the rainy season, which correlates with the beginning of the cooler season; eggs then go through a cool, dormant period of no less than 45 days, called cold torpor. In these species, embryogenesis will only start after this short, cool period. Delayed hatching and embryonic aestivation also exist in species living in arid climates, where chameleons stay in their eggs to finally hatch with the rains. This ability to delay hatching also ensures survival of the babies, allowing them to hatch at the most favorable moment, generally during the rainy season, when temperatures are neither too cold nor too hot and when the humidity is optimum.

In captivity, as the embryos in the eggs start to grow, they usually finish settling upside down, spinal cord facing the bottom part of the egg, the bellies and the umbilical cords facing the yolk which is found in the upper half of the egg. The allontois bulge fills with the waste of the

embryo standing on its backside. For this reason, baby chameleons born from eggs seem to always come out upside down.

Heat is conducted from the surface of the ground into the nest below by water, which is primarily responsible for the enzymatic reactions that take place inside the egg. However, it alone is insufficient to ensure proper hatching. Water pressure from the ground will also act on the egg and build pressure inside it that, eventually, will help the babies to break free.

In the wild, baby chameleons come out of the ground in the morning, and many hatch in the morning as well. It might take a couple of days for them to dig out of their nest if they are alone, or less time if they work their way out as a team. However, once they have made an escape route out of their nest, they disperse and stand on their own.

F. minor *hatching.*

Baby Chamaeleo jacksonii.

Live-Bearing Chameleons

Ovoviviparous chameleon species give birth to their babies four to six months after mating, in the morning during the rainy season. The number of babies ranges from six to thirty, depending on the species. At birth, the babies are expelled one by one from the female's cloaca, enclosed in a thin transparent membrane that is sticky to the touch. These membranous sacs adhere to the leaves, branches, or grass on which they are dropped and the young chamel-eons break free from them wiggling themselves out. Stillbirths can indicate a deficiency in the mother's diet.

Growth and Development

Infancy to Adulthood

Like all reptiles, chameleons grow their entire lives, a phenomenon that leads to the shedding of the outer surface of their skins. Some species, notably from the *Chamaeleo* and *Furcifer* genera, experience rapid growth as babies, maturing in three months' time. Other species from the genera *Bradypodion, Calumma,* and *Kinyongia*, and the Brookesinae, take less than a year to reach adulthood, whereas the larger species of the genus *Calumma* mature over the course of a couple years, and are considered slow growers in comparison to the fast-growing species.

Under the influence of hormones during their initial growth, baby chameleons will take on sex-specific adult morphology and colors.

Old Age

Some chamaeleonids (generally the fast-growing species) are naturally short-lived, even by lizard standards, not surviving more than a couple of years after birth. Females that breed early or intensively will also experience shorter life spans than their mates, although this phenomenon is not very well understood.

Behavioral Biology

Some chameleon behaviors are instinctual, originating from their genetic makeup, and some of their behaviors are acquired, a response to stimuli from their environments and their physiology.

Behaviors have survival, reproduction, and adaptation functions. Most

Note: Chameleon longevity depends on food very rich in powerful antioxidants and in nighttime temperature, which promote strong immune systems.

chameleon behavior, including social interactions between chameleons, is genetically programmed. The animals respond instinctually to external stimuli such as photoperiod (cycles of light and dark), light intensity and quality, relative humidity, social stimuli such as perception of colors, movements, and postures in other chameleons, and other signals (tactile, chemical, etc.).

The environments of chameleons also influence their behavior. Chameleons are able to map their territories, learn from their experiences, associate desirable outcomes with certain situations and adapt to new ones. For example, chameleons bred in captivity and accustomed to humans do not show any particular fear of their keepers. Some animals might associate the humans or their hands with food, and it's possible to imagine, under particular circumstances, that chameleons can be trained to adapt to rather different environmental conditions than the ones they would experience in the wild.

PART TWO
CHAMELEONS UNDER HUMAN CARE

Chapter Five

Chameleons in the Pet Trade

Protecting Chameleons

Chameleons have probably exerted their charms upon us for as long as there have been humans to observe them. Not long ago, the human-chameleon relationship was a story of fascination that more often than not, ended in heartbreak. Authorities thought humans' attraction to chameleons might prove fatal for the animal's survival as species in the wild, and chameleons were given protection in 1973 under an international treaty called the Convention on International Trade of Endangered Species (CITES). CITES was enacted as a means to monitor and regulate the movements between countries trading in species of plants and animals that might be threatened or endangered by predatory collection.

Problems with the Pet Trade

The pet industry has long been ostracized for its dependency on wild-caught chameleons to satisfy the human desire for this extraordinary exotic creature. True enough, the capture-related morbidity and mortality rates at exporters' facilities were high, chameleons' conditions of care and husbandry were usually guessed at rather than known, and the life histories of most of the species were not known. Only a few species were bred and established in captivity, and clutches of others failed to hatch.

Chameleons that died at the exporting facilities of operators or in the hands of hobbyists were replaced with more wild-caught chameleons, and the trade directly contributed to further removal of chameleons from the wild. It's not hard to agree with opponents of the trade and to feel sorry whenever we see pictures of stressed-out animals being caged solely for financial gain.

In the 1990s, the main exporters of wild-caught chameleons were two impoverished countries, Madagascar and Tanzania. Both countries were home to over 50 percent of the species known to date, some of which were localized or seasonal species. By the mid-90s, the growing international concern for the

Bookesia perarmata *was included in Appendix 1 of CITES because the heavy trade of the species could threaten its survival in the wild.*

plight of the species led the CITES secretariat to ask for a moratorium on the trade of many mountain species of chameleons from Tanzania; most Malagasy species of *Furcifer* (except for the eurytropic *F. lateralis*, *F. oustaleti*, *F. pardalis*, and *F. verrucosus*, which have an annual quota for export); all *Calumma* species; and *Brookesia perarmata*. Appended to CITES in 2002, the moratorium forbid the export of wild-caught specimens for commercial purposes.

Cameroon has also become a country of particular concern when it comes to chameleons. Some of its attractive species, found only in the remains of mountain forests, have been subjected to rather intense capture for the pet trade. For this reason, Cameroon has banned the export of species such as *C. pfefferi* and *C. wiedersheimi* and is likely to ban the export of other wild-caught specimens of more species in the future.

Advances in Captive Breeding

Although some chameleon populations are in serious demographic peril and some reports about chameleon welfare are legitimate cause for concern, chameleons' overall treatment continues to improve. Significant advances in chameleon management and care have led to reproductive success in several species, whereas several years ago, chameleons were deemed impossible to keep alive, let alone be bred in captivity. For those who doubt that captive breeding alone can be an effective means of species survival, let's not ignore the facts: Captive breeding programs, when properly employed, can be a great aid to preservation. A total ban on commercially bred chameleon species, on the other hand, cannot fix the problems associated with the main threat chameleons face in the wild: the use and modification of their habitats for agriculture and economic development. The simple truth is that, in some cases, if wildlife is not allowed to be bred for commercial use, there will be no more of this wildlife left in the not-so-distant future.

It is especially important that the pet industry and hobbyists alike address the remaining weaknesses in chameleon management and care, and build their case for keeping the right to care for their animals. There are ethical, legal, practical, public relations, and other issues to consider, and concerned parties should position themselves to become part of the solution, instead of letting some animal-rights lobbies depict them as part

Find Out More on the Web

http://chameleonnews.com
http://www.adcham.com
http://www.melleridiscovery.com

of the problem. It is, indeed, critical that the pet industry and hobbyists recognize their vulnerabilities and attempt to address them proactively, rather than losing control over their right to keep and breed their animals.

Here are some tips for the responsible chameleon owner or enthusiast:

- Know where to find valid information.
- Join a group online (beginner to specialist).
- If you are not familiar with keeping chameleons, consider starting with a Veiled chameleon.
- Captive-bred chameleons are always preferable to wild-caught chameleons for a number of reasons.
- Locate dependable live food and multivitamin/mineral suppliers, or be your own invertebrate breeder if you're not sure you can rely on anyone else.
- Work out a budget for housing, lighting, heating, watering, feeding, and terrarium decoration.
- Have equipment ready to house your animals.
- Donate to and/or participate in groups supporting your chameleon hobby or business.

Chapter Six
Keeping Chameleons

Chameleons might be seen as "high-maintenance" animals by reptile keepers. I only partially agree with this statement. I believe that chameleons are no more high-maintenance than some types of monitor lizards, parrots and birds of prey, or certain poison dart frogs. In any case, I strongly believe they are worth the extra effort you might put into making them comfortable. One way the animals might repay your efforts is by breeding and giving you another generation of chameleons.

Unfortunately, the majority of equipment currently found in pet stores does not adequately address the real needs of most reptiles that people intend to keep. Do your research and seek out professional websites and breeders for ideas and equipment before running out and making an uninformed purchase.

Tips for Purchasing Your Chameleon

If you are not familiar with chameleons, or if this is the first time you are acquiring one, do some research, join a chameleon hobbyist group, prepare your chameleon's environment, and start with a captive-bred specimen of an easy-to-find species, such as the Veiled or Panther chameleon.

Most Commonly Kept Species

Of all the chameleon species kept under human care, the Veiled chameleon is the most common. There are two major reasons for this:

1. The species is comfortable with the low relative humidity (RH) of a household (50 to 65 percent under normal circumstances).

2. Babies are readily available as captive-bred specimens.

Attention!

In all cases, the importance of researching the animal you intend to keep (its scientific name, origin, habitat, natural history, biology, etc.) cannot be emphasized enough. Take advantage of the World Wide Web, libraries, magazines, and clubs to make sure you are well informed.

These two factors alone explain the extraordinary rise in popularity of this species. Another species, the Panther chameleon (*Furcifer pardalis*), requires a higher RH, but may live satisfactorily with an RH around 65 percent. This is why they fare well in a heavily planted cage with frequent misting.

If you are a bit more familiar with keeping chameleons, you might want to try a different species. Wild-caught chameleons are usually a poor choice; as a breeder, I believe that going for captive-bred animals is always wiser. Few species aside from the Veiled and Panther chameleons are currently being bred in large numbers, but private breeders are getting better at breeding some new species. In time, more captive-bred species of chameleons should become available.

You should always perform a quick visual examination on the animal(s) you have decided to adopt. If you can't see the animal in person before purchasing it, ask for pictures. Ideally, the animal should be plump, the vertebrae not clearly visible, the skin and scalation undamaged, the toes and the tail intact, and the eyes open and not sunken in their sockets. The grip of the animal should be firm, and it should be able to stand by itself. Make sure to hydrate the animal upon arrival at your home and to offer it some fresh, live insects.

Caring for Chameleons

When you decide to become the keeper of one or more chameleons, you are taking on the responsibility of giving the best care to your animal(s). Other than basic care, I would like to address two additional issues here. One is stress, and the other is environment enrichment. Chameleons are notorious for being easily stressed, and everything should be done to eliminate or lessen stress factors. On the other hand, chameleons also enjoy a bit of excitement in their everyday lives, and keepers should ensure their animals' well-being through enrichment.

Stress Reduction

Stress comes in two types: physiological and psychological. Physiological stress affects the body, causing pain to the animal—for example, too-high temperatures, illness, etc. Psychological stress comes from the mental pressure that

Chameleons from serious breeders are a good bet for the first time pet owner.

Although animals are able to handle short-term stressors, chronic situations causing long-term stress will cause their bodies to release the hormone cortisol, which suppresses the immune system, inducing higher rates of infection and illnesses. Cortisol also clamps down on the reproductive functions, reducing libido and reproductive hormones. If you are keeping chameleons, too much stress will be counterproductive to your objectives, causing illness in your animals and decreasing your success in breeding them.

If you are offering your animals an adequate environment and health care, it can be assumed that their physiological stress is low or nonexistent, and you are starting off on the right foot.

Chameleons are psychological animals, and they instinctively have things to worry about, such as getting eaten, beaten up, or not getting enough food or drink. It is your responsibility to keep these worries out of your lizards' minds. Chameleons will also look for comfort in things like basking spots, sex, and food treats, but you can bring them a great deal of comfort and enjoyment with environment enrichment, which is the provision of stimuli encouraging natural behavior in chameleons, such as communication display, basking, food foraging, etc.

Environmental Enrichment

Chameleon behaviors can be classified as resting, pattern cruising (repetitive or recurrent patrolling), ran-

is put on the animals (such as being bullied by others, or depressed by a lack of light or rough handling).

Physiological stress is obvious when chameleons look hurt or in bad shape, when they are panting, or when they show abnormal coloration or behavior. Psychological stress can be suspected when the animals are scared: they hide, stay prostrated, or show submissive coloration (black or very dark under normal climatic conditions for most species). They may also display obvious discomfort with their surroundings ("window crawling" or trying to find an escape route from their habitat).

Calumma malthe *(female) being irritated by a pushy male. Beware of stress.*

dom cruising (exploring), focused behavior, courtship, aggression, hiding, orientation, and non-categorized behavior. When environment enrichment is available to chameleons, and stress is reduced to its minimum, random cruising, courtship, and focused behaviors increase, whereas hiding (including submissive coloration), resting, and pattern cruising decrease.

In a nutshell, if you are going to keep chameleons, you need to eliminate the stress factors and to ensure their environment is also fun to explore.

Whenever you can, start with captive-bred animals. Captive-bred animals are not always problem- or disease-free, but they are used to humans as a natural aspect of their surroundings, they are usually less likely to harbor parasites, and are usually young animals (so you know what to expect in terms of life span).

If you cannot start with captive-bred animals, start with young wild-caught specimens. While designing and building your chameleon enclosure, bear in mind what your animals need for both activity and comfort. When stress is kept to an acceptable level and their environment is rich in stimuli, chameleons are sure to fare better and reproduce with ease.

Creating the Best Environment

You may keep your chameleons in terrariums or in outdoors enclosures. From what we have explored about their needs, likes, and habits, chameleons primarily require access to heat, visible light, and UV radiation.

Chameleons also need an environment with the proper relative humidity for their age and species. I mention age because babies might have different requirements than adults.

Panther chameleon in an outdoor cage.

Chameleons need a reasonable variety of live food (preferably invertebrates) and micro- (vitamins and minerals) and macronutrients (proteins, fats, sugars) to grow. Some small captive-bred vertebrates (lizards, geckos, pinky mice, birds) can be added for medium and larger species of chameleons.

Chameleons need a space to feel comfortable. They will use this space for their general well-being (physical and emotional) as well as to drink, eat, bask, and meet and retreat from other beings or uncomfortable climatic factors. Whether you keep your animals outside or inside, you must create a closed environment that is adequate and safe for them. Temperature, humidity, and light should be your primary concerns.

The walls of the space where you keep your animals will most likely be solid—glass, acrylic, brick, and wood panel are a few of the possibilities—and allow some exchange with the outside world (heat, airflow, light, RH). The greater the flow between your enclosure (whether outdoor or indoor) and the outside environment, the more difficult it is to control the conditions inside the enclosure.

Keeping Chameleons Outside

The very first thing to do if you want to keep chameleons outside is to take some climatic measurements. On hot days and cold days, record the low and high temperatures and the RH of the area you are thinking about using to house your animals, and compare them to the data relative to the habitat where your chameleon's are naturally found. The great thing about using natural sunlight for your animals is the free irradiations you get (infrared,

Understanding UV Rays

Ultraviolet rays come in three kinds, A, B, and C. Ultraviolet A (UVA) and ultraviolet B (UVB) are electromagnetic wavelengths ranging from 400 nanometers to 315 nanometers and are responsible for stimulating the parietal eye in chameleons. This, in turn, prompts the release of hormones by the hypothalamus and the regulation of various biological activities linked to growth, food intake, follicle production, and breeding behavior. UVB radiations are electromagnetic wavelengths in the range of 315 to 290 nanometers. UVB irradiation is important in chameleons for metabolizing provitamin D_3 to vitamin D_3, which is responsible for proper bone construction and embryo viability. Depriving chameleons of UVB irradiation leads to stunted growth, rickets, soft bones (metabolic bone disease or MBD), and low egg-hatching success.

visible light, and UV radiations). If the climatic conditions are just right, you might be able to keep some species outside in mesh cages, but if the disparity between the outside climate and the desired temperature and RH is too great, you might have to shape the landscape, and make use of more materials and equipment, to keep your animals healthy.

Outside netted greenhouse for chameleons.

A major drawback of keeping animals outside is the risk of them getting lost, attacked, or preyed upon by other animals, not to mention theft. You might want to build a wildlife-proof setup to protect your chameleons from birds, rats, raccoons, snakes, and cats.

However, the advantages of keeping your chameleons outdoors are numerous. The sun's rays are free, for starters, and a well-designed enclosure offers more opportunities for the animals to find their comfort zones and display naturalistic behavior—and for you to enjoy the show.

It is beyond the scope of this book to address all the building and landscaping issues you might encounter in designing an area with the kind of microclimate your chameleons need. However, here are a few general considerations. If you opt for a walk-in or pass-through enclosure or green-

house, use common sense and seek the help of professionals.

It's a good idea to use materials that will keep pests out and your chameleons safe. If you plan to use plants and a lot of water, ensure proper drainage to avoid suffocating the roots of the plants and muddying the entire area. Herbs and plants can be used for decoration, hanging perches, and as food sources for insects (tomatoes for tomato hornworms, mulberry for silkworms, grass for locusts), and flowers attract pollinating insects (including flies). Keep in mind, though, that some plants might be toxic to the animals (some chameleons eat leaves and chew on branches). If you are going to use electric equipment, ensure it is weather- and waterproof and that any switches sit outside of the wet area.

Environment Enrichment

Environment enrichment is the provision of diverse stimuli to promote the expression of species-specific chameleon behavior. For that purpose, enclosures can be fitted with natural elements (vines, pools, basking spots, wet areas, walkways, spots for observing).

Master Plan and Design

Volume of the enclosure: Try to allow as much space as possible for your animals. Chameleons tend to be more active when given space to roam around.

The four quadrants: Split the cage space into four overlapping

Ideas for Environment Enrichment

- Tunnels and walkways to other parts of the enclosure (male chameleons love to cruise these walkways in search of females)
- Plants in the middle of a pond (where chameleons can roost)
- Basking spots (facing east or south, or right in front of metal halide lights)
- Shower/fogging spots (a great favorite of mountain chameleons)
- Dry spots
- Feeding spots (with silkworms or flies)
- Mirrors (These are fine in large enclosures as chameleons do not feel threatened by their own reflection. Some aggressive species such as *F. pardalis* love to come face to face with their own reflections)
- Hiding spots
- Insectary plants (plants that attract insects) and beneficial insects (silkworms, lacewings, hoverflies, as well as other flying insects) in your outdoor enclosure (crawling insects might try to get out of sight, so it is best to offer these in feeding stations where they cannot hide)
- Special treats (green cockroaches, *Panchlora nivea*, tomato hornworms, or praying mantises) on occasion (you can train your chameleons with food rewards)

Furcifer lateralis major *(female).*

areas: sunny/shady on either half of the south-north line and dry/humid in the east and west, respectively. You should then have four quadrants: sunny/dry, sunny/humid, shady/dry, and shady/humid. Let your chameleons choose their favorite spots.

Solar exposure: Morning sunlight is usually what chameleons use to warm themselves up, so make sure the morning sun reaches inside your cage for your creatures' comfort. The afternoon sun is typically the hottest and not useful to chameleons that are getting ready to sleep. If you have to build a wall for your enclosure, make sure it faces west.

Soil and landscape: You should talk to a landscape specialist when choosing your soil. Different soils have different properties in terms of heat and water retention, and many females are very finicky when it comes to a laying spot, often favoring loamy soils.

Spatial design: Chameleons either live among dead plant material on the ground (*Brookesia* spp.), on vertical branches (stump-tailed), or on horizontal branches (typical chameleons). Make sure to add vines and branches that fall both vertically and horizontally in the four quadrants. Also be sure to make escape routes to dead ends, as well as potential hiding spots for your animals. When you are setting up the plants, branches, and other features of your enclosure, be sure to avoid wires and anything that might get tangled in the animals' tongues.

Watering and sprinkling systems: These work best when situated on the upper part of the enclosure, as animals like to get showers and lap falling water from leaves. Make use of lead-free products designed for humans to avoid possible poisoning of your animals over the long term.

The Different Types of Outside Enclosures

Warm and Dry Weather: Mesh cage The mesh should be strong enough to deter rats, raccoons, errant family dogs, and other wildlife. It should also be fine enough to keep food insects from getting out. Bury the foundation of the structure deep in the ground to prevent rats from intruding, and avoid wood frames, which might easily rot.

Temperature control: Plants (especially some palm trees) can buffer heat by water evaporation. Shade nets *outside* of the enclosure, made out of aluminum and mounted on short-grass slopes facing south and west can help transmit valuable light while stopping some of the heat. Misting or fogging in dry areas will dissipate the heat through water evaporation and cool down the air.

RH control: The RH of your enclosure can be slightly increased by frequent misting or the addition of a waterfall, sprinklers, water pond, or streams in and/or around the area and at the bottom of the slopes facing the cages. Where soil moisture is a problem, construct a French drain filled with pea-sized gravel to keep the water below the surface. You can also utilize a perforated drain tile to catch water and carry it to an outlet.

Light: Beware of the photoperiod (length of day), as it varies seasonally in relation to your distance from the equator. Light can be subdued with shades and blinds, and weatherproof metal halide floodlights can be used as a substitute for sunlight.

The cage can face southeast and possibly west; it is safe to build a wall on the northern side. A wet wall of bricks on which plants are grown can considerably cool the area, too.

Hot and Dry Weather: Cooling greenhouse Cool, evaporative greenhouses are expensive to buy and to run, but if you are a serious breeder or keeper living in a hot, dry climate, they are an excellent option for keeping a large group of animals. The foundation of the greenhouse can be made out of bricks to prevent intruders.

Temperature control: External air is sucked through a cooling panel at one end of the greenhouse by powerful fans at the other end of the greenhouse. The evaporation of water running on the panel ensures the humidification of the air and a considerable drop in heat.

RH control: In a cool, evaporative greenhouse, the humidity can be as high as 90 percent, but the temperature can be significantly lower than the outside. If you need a lower RH, you will need to make use of desiccating machines or salts. This kind of greenhouse only works in hot and dry environments and is ideal for rainforest species.

Light: Photoperiods vary seasonally in relation to your distance from the equator, but chameleons always need a minimum daily exposure of ten hours of daylight. If UV transmission is an issue, be sure to use vitamin D supplements in your animals' food. You can also use an extra shading screen on the western part of the unit to protect against over-heating.

Cool Weather: Greenhouse
Some keepers house chameleons in greenhouses. Make sure not to use insecticides on your greenhouse plants or you might kill your animals.

Temperature control: It is easy to overheat a greenhouse, so take precautions here. If you can invest in a thermostat to control the temperature in your greenhouse, by all means do it. A greenhouse should always be oriented north-south to avoid fast overheating.

RH control: Humidity basically depends on how much water has been added inside the greenhouse versus how much air ventilation comes from the outside. The RH can be monitored with a hygrostat linked to an automatic sprinkling system.

Light: For the greenhouse panels, make sure to use an acrylic glass, such as Solacryl, that transmits UV radiations. Glass and many plastic materials will filter UVB out, in which case, you might need to supplement your chameleons' food with vitamin D and possibly use full-spectrum UVB lamps positioned at a proper distance from the animals.

Feeding and Watering in Outside Enclosures

It's a good idea to introduce some invertebrates (insects and other prey, like farm-bred snails to avoid introducing parasites to your animals) in your enclosure before setting the chameleons inside. You can also release a few caterpillars or

Find Out More on the Web

http://chameleonnews.com/ ?page=article&id=77

cockroaches, put some crickets in baskets easily accessible to the chameleons, or let a few gut-loaded flies in from time to time when you visit your pets. Based on my own experience, chameleons are experts at finding their food in such surroundings.

For watering purposes, you can use automatic gardening drip systems. Keep in mind that you should always use nontoxic, human-grade plastic material for the tubing and the equipment.

C. quadricornis (male) roosting on the misting system's pipeline.

Chapter Seven

Keeping Chameleons Indoors

If you are going to keep your chameleons inside your home, you may want to allocate a full room to this purpose. It all depends on how many animals you have, the species, and your goals. The room might just be for cages housing your animals, their food insects and the equipment needed for your hobby, but it can also serve a larger purpose: a free-range room.

Free-range Rooms

The purpose of a free-range room is twofold. First, it is meant to keep your chameleons happier than if kept in a cage. Second, with a bit of planning, it is like a walk-in aviary, except with chameleons!

If you are keeping a good number of animals, if you are trying to give your animals as much comfort as you can, or if you are keeping large species of adult animals, then the free-range room might be the right concept for you. In general, I think cages should be as large and as comfortable as possible for the animals, so that they do not feel encaged. (If you are keeping animals with aggressive tendencies, you'll need to include sight barriers in the room to avoid stressing the other chameleons.)

Where the room should be is up to you. Many breeders choose the basement for convenience and for the fact that the temperature and relative humidity underground are more stable. Some houses don't have basements, so attics are another possibility for breeders, allowing them to keep their animals away from common living areas. However, a garage, a garden shed or a small room anywhere is enough.

Designing a Free-range Room

When it comes to the design of a free-range room, it is a good idea to have one regular door opening out from the room and a screen door that closes from the inside to the outside. This setup allows you to ventilate the room without risking a chameleon escape; it is also a safety measure for the animals inside the room should you forget to shut the main door or leave it ajar.

C. quadricornis *(female) in a free-range room.*

Since you are going to use the room as a chameleon facility, it will need a bit of planning. To start with, you'll need to insulate the walls and possibly the ceiling. Because water will be used in the room, think about protecting the walls with a very good paint and possibly installing a slanted tile floor for water drainage. Address the issue any way you see fit, but a word of caution here: Don't just go for the cheap alternatives. They always turn out to be the most expensive ones in the long run.

You will need some electrical components (lights at least), so make sure of a few things:

- Get an electrician (or at least someone who knows what he is doing) to do the job for you.

- Use weather-proof equipment.
- Use a ground fault circuit interrupter outlet for your electrical equipment.
- Place the control switches outside of the room.
- If possible, automate everything.

Lighting

You can hang lamps from the ceiling or affix them to the walls, but in any case, use marine or outdoor equipment. Metal halide projectors should be weatherproof. Their technology will give you the maximum light output than any other light source, including a lot of UVA and UVB. You should make use of bulbs of no less than 400 watts (as projectors) with a 5,500 Kelvin degree color rendition in a free-range room. They last much longer than many other lamps and are, in my opinion, the best option when it comes to artificial lighting for chameleons.

Some mercury vapor lamps emit too much UV radiation and may endanger the lives and the eyes of your animals. I have heard of some safer mercury vapor lamps, but I only use metal halides and natural sunshine for my own chameleons. You might want to look into hydroponics equipment and facilities, or scour the Web for more information on equipment and setup. Instead of metal halides, some keepers use fluorescent lamps hanging from above (Zoo Med ReptiSun 10.0, for example). The basking site must be six to twelve inches away from the

Important Note

There are some things you must consider before creating a free-range room for your animals. Because you will need water sprinklers and electrical equipment in it (for temperature and light control), you must be very careful with the electricity setup and maintenance. If you are not an electrician, seek professional help.

lamp, however, and other hot spots must also be provided. Users of fluorescent lamps have to be mindful of splashes of water, which can blow out the bulb. Fluorescent lamps lose their UVB output power as they are used, and need to be replaced every six months or so. Weatherproof metal halide lamps, on the other hand, will, watt for watt, give you forty times more light output than any fluorescent, as well as the heat you need on cold days.

Plants and Walking Areas

The plants you put in your room will be better left in their pots. They will be easier to move around and to replace if necessary. Remember that you will also need to be able to reach pretty much every part of the room. Chameleons might be climbing creatures, but they also like to stand and cruise on horizontal planes. Horizontal branches and vines are meant for this, so don't just go for plants with vertical branches. You should place several twigs and branches in front of the metal halides lamps, as they will

Baby Panther chameleons in an acrylic terrarium to keep the RH at the desired level.

be used as basking spots by your chameleon. In years of experimenting with such setups and keeping hundreds of chameleons this way, I have never seen a chameleon burning him/herself against the lights, unlike other heat lamps that have scalded so many pets. One thing chameleons seem to find hard to resist are the water pipes you will use for your misting system. Keep this in mind when designing your free-range room, as a lot of chameleons are likely to use them as pathways, roosting spots, and meeting perches.

Furcifer labordi (male) bred under human supervision sleeping in his ventilated cage.

Temperature Control

Depending on the climate where you live and the requirements of the species you are keeping, you may need to adjust the temperature to suit your animal's needs. You may need to install an air conditioner if you reside in a very hot climate. In cooler climates, you may need to install a thermostat-controlled space heater. (The best types are oil-filled radiators.) Here are some examples:

- **You live in a hot climate, and you are keeping mountain and forest chameleons.**

You will need a well-insulated room with air conditioning. You might want to use an ultrasonic humidifying machine to raise the RH in your room to the desirable level, as the AC will considerably dry the atmosphere.

- **You live in a cold climate, and you are keeping mountain and plateau chameleons.**

The heat generated by the metal halides in your room will encourage your chameleons to bask and heat themselves. Well insulated with the proper RH gradient, the room should allow for the necessary night drop in temperature to keep your chameleons healthy.

- **You live in a temperate region, and you are keeping Veiled chameleons.**

An oil-filled space heater will warm your chameleons by air convection. This is suitable (if not necessary) for Veiled chameleons, as they live in hot regions.

You should also pay attention to the room's location. It is always best to properly insulate the walls and to use a basement room where the temperature is cooler, rather than a non-insulated attic or a room with southwestern exposure, which would overheat very quickly in summertime with the lights on. You might want to use a fan with an exhaust duct for the heat. Also be mindful that many chameleons will find their way inside small holes or pipes. Plan and design accordingly.

Jackson's chameleon drinking from the misted water in its cage.

Water and Relative Humidity

Your animals receive water from their atmosphere and when you sprinkle it onto them. Although sprinkling water will temporarily raise the ambient RH in the air, it might not be sufficient to keep your animals healthy, especially if you use an air conditioning system in the room.

It is, therefore, a good idea to invest in at least one (if not two, for a large room) large ultrasonic humidifier. You can easily replace the fog duct with a high PVC pipe with "L" or "T" shaped ends to direct the fog wherever you would like to raise the humidity. Very often, you will spot your chameleons resting right under the fog. If you need to keep the room at a rather high and uniform relative humidity, you might use fans to disperse the fog around the room.

Attention!

Sprinkling water in a hot room—75°F (27°C) and over—will cause a bacterial infection on the skin of your animals (pseudomonal infection) that might lead to systemic infection and death if left untreated. Sprinkle water in a room where the air is not hotter than 71°F (21°C) to avoid this problem.

Automatic Controls

If you can afford it, you should automize switches, solenoid valves, and thermostats and put them on timers.

Chameleons usually like to lick water drops rather than drink from standing water (although they also do it). For this reason, you might want to install a drip system. Water bottles for laboratory animals work well, as the chameleons are attracted to the shine of the little ball from the watering tube and soon learn how to get water from it if you show them how to proceed. Or, you might decide to go for a more natural setup with misting nozzles. For this system to work, you need filtered (reverse osmosis) water, a water reservoir, and a pump to produce the pressure needed to vaporize the water through the nozzles. If your water is not too hard and not too laden with chemicals, you can use an automatic garden watering system with a regular 80 PSI pressurized pump (the kind used for home reverse osmosis water treatment systems).

Feeding

Some breeders place feeding stations here and there in their setups, whereas others let the animals forage for their food. In the latter case, it is a good idea to ensure that your animals are eating healthy invertebrates, so as to avoid possible parasitic transmission.

Find Out More on the Web

www.instructables.com/id/ A-Free-Range-Habitat-for- Mellers-and-other-Large-/

Some chameleons enjoy having baths.

Chapter Eight

Keeping Chameleons in Terrariums

Chameleons can be caged or kept in terrariums. In fact, babies should be kept this way until they are large enough to be moved into larger spaces. In a too-large space, babies might not be able to find their food easily. The concept of the terrarium is a spatial volume meant to keep specific species in the right environmental conditions.

As seen before, the three major climatic parameters of an artificial biotope are temperature, humidity, and light. The greater the enclosure's exchange with and differential in parameters with its surroundings, the more difficult it is to maintain the desired conditions.

Terrariums or Cages?

There has been debate about keeping chameleons in glass terrariums versus keeping them in screened cages that allow a lot more airflow. Glass terrariums should not be mistaken for glass tanks or fish tanks that keep the air stale and the humidity high. Popular in Europe, they are usually well ventilated and are meant to help keep a certain level of internal humidity and stable temperatures with the help of special equipment (humidifiers, misting systems). Glass terrariums for chameleons usually have sliding doors on the front with a mesh section placed on the bottom and another one on the back of the terrarium or on its roof. Air may be forced in or sucked out with fans, depending on the atmosphere of the room where the terrariums are kept.

Screened cages, on the other hand, are more popular in the United States, where, in general, the equipment for keeping chameleons is more simplistic and may consist of simply a light, a heating bulb, a drip system, and a mesh cage furnished with plants and vines. The major drawback of the screened cage is that it does not allow much temperature and humidity control and is subject to air drafts. It can be convenient for some of the hardy species (Common, Veiled, and Panther chameleons), but you need to control climatic parameters in the room for

species requiring specific microclimatic conditions.

Some breeders make cages out of cupboards or plastic panels with fans on the back, with just one glass window in the front, while others explore other possibilities. In some hot countries, keeping cool-climate species of chameleons is challenging, and some breeders (like me) have to resort to air conditioning of some sort, either in the terrarium or outside of the cages, to keep the animals at their preferred air temperature.

Size

The minimum size of a chameleon terrarium or cage should be based on the adult size of the animals being kept—usually the larger the better. To find the bare minimum, let's use the length of an adult animal as a benchmark, and call that length L, or $2L$ for a pair of chameleons. Interior dimensions can be calculated as follows based on the size of one animal (double the figures for a pair):

- Width = $2 \times L$
- Length = $4 \times L$
- Height = $3 \times L$

Example: A pair of Jackson's chameleons (*Chamaeleo jacksonii*) each 9 inches long (23 cm), would

need a terrarium 3 feet wide (90 cm), 6 feet long (183 cm), and 54 inches high (140 cm).

Light

Artificial lighting in a terrarium for chamaeleonids can be achieved with several types of light sources:
- Metal halides
- Fluorescent lamps
- Mercury vapor lamps
- Incandescent lamps

Metal Halides

Metal halides are high-technology lights that will give you the most light for your buck. These all-in-one lights are extremely useful if you are keeping chameleons, as you will not have to buy several types of lamps (UVA, UVB, visible light, heat bulb). They are by far your best option, as they most closely resemble sunlight. They can be used with all species of chameleons, and they are an absolute necessity if you are keeping species that do not necessarily dwell in evergreen forests (sciophilous species)—for example, prairie, plateau, and deciduous forest species. Metal halide lamps work best for heliophilic (sun-loving) species of chameleons. In order to be efficient, the lights have to stay relatively close to the animals—10 inches (25 cm) at the *closest* for a 400-watt bulb. Metal halides and their ballasts give off quite a bit of heat, and this is something you should keep in mind if you are building your own enclosures.

Other breeders prefer to make use of screened cages, but often use metal halides as lighting features.

Avoiding Electrical Accidents

It is important to use caution when handling electrical equipment and wiring, which are particularly hazardous when used in connection with water. Always observe the following safeguards carefully:

• Before using any of the electrical equipment described in this book, check to be sure that it carries the UL safety symbol.

• Use waterproof lamps or keep them away from water or spray.

• Before using any equipment in water, check the label to make sure it is suitable for underwater use.

• Disconnect the main electrical plug before you begin any work in a water terrarium or touch any equipment.

• Be sure the electric current passes through a central fuse box or circuit breaker system. Such a system should only be installed by a licensed electrician.

Note: Make sure to follow the instructions for the installation and use of this equipment!

Fluorescent

Fluorescents are not as bright or elaborate as metal halides (40 times less light, watt for watt). They are cheaper, but they do not last as long, and they as well as their ballasts can also give off quite a bit of heat. They need to be placed rather close to the animals to get the full benefit of their UV radiations. Some newer models, such as Zoo Med ReptiSun 10.0 provide sufficient UVB, even for species requiring high exposure, if positioned between six to twelve inches from the animal and mounted on a metal reflector. Fluorescent bulbs should be replaced every six months or so. You'll need to purchase a UVB meter to monitor the lamps' rates of decline, as they vary greatly from bulb to bulb, even within the same brand. Most keepers pair them with heat bulbs so that the chameleons, being attracted to the heat, also get their daily dose of UVB.

Fluorescents should mainly be used for forest and mountain species.

Mercury Vapor and Incandescent

Mercury vapor lamps and incandescent bulbs are usually not good options in enclosures for chameleons. Mercury vapor lamps might emit too much UV radiation for the physical well-being of the animals, and most of the wattage from incandescent light is dissipated away in heat. The incandescent light spectrum is also notoriously imbalanced; if you are using incandescent, you will need to accommodate for the chamaeleonids' UVA and UVB needs with some fluorescent lamps as well.

I recommend that serious breeders invest in metal halides.

Heating and Temperature Control

Chameleons draw their body heat either from radiations or from air conduction.

In the African mountains, for example, the surrounding air might be cool, but the intense sun rays provide the heat chameleons need to warm themselves. On the other hand, species living in hot environments, like *C. calyptratus*, *F. pardalis*, and *F. oustaleti*, fare better if the surrounding atmosphere is rather hot as they draw heat from air conduction.

This chameleon has its own cage, a feeding dish, a hot spot (halogen), UVA, UVB and more visible light are provided by the means of a specific flourescent tube. This kind of set up is pretty standard and works satisfactorily for hardy species.

Important Note

In any enclosure, it is necessary to provide thermal gradients for your animals—that is, cooler and hotter areas. Create some hot spots in your enclosure as well as some shady/moist areas where passive evaporation (by air convection, for example) will reduce heat.

Chameleons cool off in the shade, or by roosting on a branch, where air convection and water evaporation allow for more comfortable temperatures.

Ambient Room Temperature

Whether you are using a glass terrarium or a screened cage, make sure that the ambient temperature doesn't exceed the average temperature preferred by the species you are intending to keep. Glass terrariums used to keep cool-weather species in hot climates are available, but unless you are familiar with miniature air conditioners, you would be better off with a fully air-conditioned room if the ambient temperature is too hot to keep the intended species.

Relative Humidity

Relative humidity in terrariums can be controlled by adding water through misting systems, ultrasonic humidifying machines (cold foggers), and evaporative systems.

Misting systems consist of a water supply (a tank or direct connecting pipe tapping into filtered [reverse osmosis] or municipality water), and a pump to pressurize the water and force it into pipes and nozzles that mist the plants and animals. Misting systems can be installed in large and small enclosures, as well as free-range rooms, and left to work on automatic mode. They can be put to good use in all glass terrariums and screened cages.

Ultrasonic humidifiers (also called cold foggers because they do not heat the water to vaporize it) are best used during the nighttime in cool Afromontane screened cages (ensuring 100 percent RH in the cage) and in the morning in Sudanese and Sudano-Guinean screen cages, as they simulate the morning dew. (See the descriptions of different cage types below.)

Passive evaporative systems work with glass terrariums and rely on the amount of water available, heat radiation, air convection, and the plants living in the terrarium to modify the degree of humidity. In a nutshell, this is how the system works:

1. Select a terrarium with ventilation on both the bottom and the top.

2. Fill the bottom part with hydroponic clay balls. A thick capillary matting of some sort which draws water upwards should be laid on the clay balls.

3. Set potted plants, branches, and vines inside the terrarium and then add water until it wets the mat.

4. You can sow seeds of flowers or plants and leave them to germinate with the help of a metal halide lamp set in the ceiling of the glass terrarium. The seeds will root in the fabric.

5. The heat given off by the metal halide lamp will cause some water to evaporate through the ventilation on the roof, and air convection will bring the cooler air from below inside the terrarium. As the plants grow, they will provide more shade and participate, through water evaporation, in cooling the unit.

6. Humidity can be controlled by adding water to the terrarium, or not replacing the evaporated water.

Active evaporative systems work on the same principles, except that the air convection is forced with the help of 12-volt DC fans (the type used in computer cooling systems).

Plants and Substrates

Plants and substrates also play a part in regulating the humidity in the

Attention!
When selecting plants, keep in mind that many species of true chameleons will forage on plants around them. The reason for this is not very well known. Some chameleons go for the bark, hanging dead leaves or fresh ones, and flowers. It is therefore of utmost importance that the plants you choose to put in your enclosures be nontoxic, and, preferably, edible.

A greenhouse with a variety of tropical plants.

enclosure. The plants provide cover for the animals and are certainly pleasing to the eye as well. Terrarium plants flourish under metal halide lighting. Horizontal branches should be provided at different levels so animals have ample space to exercise. For naturalistic terrariums, a layer of soil can be used to support shade-loving plants, although far better future results will be obtained by incorporating new technologies.

Ventilation

If a screened cage is allowing too much airflow, some of the screen panels can be covered with clear plastic or acrylic. In a glass terrarium, airflow is governed by convection (hot air is carried away and replaced by cooler air drafted from the surroundings through the bottom of the terrarium). Air can also be moved, sucked out, or forced in by a thermostat-controlled 12-volt fan.

Special Equipment

Many kinds of electric timers, thermostats, misting systems, and cooling devices can be used to adjust the climatic parameters of your enclosures. It is beyond the scope of this book to look into the possibilities of the current technology, but this is something you should explore on your own. Luckily, a lot of information is available on the Internet for those who look for it.

Different Types of Cages and Terrariums

Terrariums and chameleon cages can be classified into many categories. I classify them according to the type of climate they are meant to replicate. The Sudanese, Sudano-Guinean, and forest-edge types are "hot" terrariums, meaning that some areas in the terrariums can reach 92°F (33.3°C); the forest and rainforest terrariums are transitional forms between the "hot" and the "cool" terrariums; and the "cool" terrariums are the plateau and mountainous types, where the temperature must not exceed 82°F (28°C) at the hottest spots.

All terrariums should offer temperature and humidity gradients, with some areas being on the cooler, moister, shadier side, and others on the drier, hotter, sunnier side. Also, many chamaeleonids in the wild experience night drops of temperatures, even by just a few degrees. Desert, plateau, and mountain species experience the largest drops in temperature, which can be signifi-

Types of Cages or Terrariums

Enclosure	Species
Sudanese	*C. calcaricarens, C. calyptratus, C. namaquensis, C. zeylanicus*
Sudano-Guinean	*Furcifer antimena, F. oustaleti, F. verrucosus*
Forest Edge	*Furcifer labordi, F. pardalis, C. gracilis, C. oweni, C. quilensis*
Plateau	*Furcifer campani, F. lateralis, F. minor*
Equatorial Rainforest	*Chamaeleo cristatus, Chamaeleo gracilis*
Tropical Rainforest	*Calumma gastrotaenia, Calumma parsonii, Furcifer balteatus, F. bifidus*
Afromontane	*C. deremensis, C. jacksonii, C. johnstoni, C. quadricornis, Kinyongia fisheri*
Afro-alpine	*Chamaeleo johnstoni, Kinyongia xenorhina, Rhampholeon acuminatus, C. hoehnelii*

Regional Climatic Data

Period	1st–6th month	7th–9th month	10th–12th month
Sudanese			
Photoperiod	11–14 hours	10–11 hours	10–14 hours
Relative Humidity	65%–75%	50%–65%	35%–40%
Temperature	76–84°F (25–29°C)	74–78°F (24–26°C)	78–88°F (26–32°C)
Sudano-Guinean			
Photoperiod	11–14 hours	10–11 hours	10–14 hours
Relative Humidity	75%–85%	50%–65%	40%
Temperature	74–84°F (24–29°C)	72–78°F (22–26°C)	78–88°F (26–32°C)
Forest Edge			
Photoperiod	12–13 hours	10–11 hours	10–13 hours
Relative Humidity	75%–80%	70%–75%	75%
Temperature	74–79°F (24–27°C)	72–78°F (22–26°C)	78–84°F (26–29°C)
Plateau			
Photoperiod	12–13 hours	10–11 hours	10–13 hours
Relative Humidity	75%–80%	70%–75%	75%
Temperature	74–84°F (24–29°C)	60–72°F (15–22°C)	72–79°F (22–27°C)
Tropical Rainforest			
Photoperiod	12–13 hours	10–11 hours	10–13 hours
Relative Humidity	75%–90%	75%–80%	75%
Temperature	74–82°F (24–28°C)	69–78°F (20–26°C)	78–84°F (26–29°C)
Subtropical Afromontane			
Photoperiod	12–13 hours	10–11 hours	10–13 hours
Relative Humidity	80%–100%	75%–85%	75%–85%
Temperature	66–80°F (19–27°C)	61–72°F (16–22°C)	72–78°F (22–26°C)

Regional Climatic Data (continued)

Period	1st–4th month	5th–8th month	9th–12th month
Equatorial Rainforest			
Photoperiod	12 hours constant	12 hours constant	12 hours constant
Relative Humidity	80%–90%	75%–80%	75%
Temperature	74–82°F (24–28°C)	72–78°F (22–26°C)	78–82°F (26–28°C)
Equatorial Afromontane			
Photoperiod	12 hours constant	12 hours constant	12 hours constant
Relative Humidity	80%–90%	75%–80%	75%
Temperature	72–80°F (22–27°C)	66–78°F (19–26°C)	68–82°F (20–28°C)

Chamaeleo feae *in an equatorial, afromontane terrarium.*

Calumma gastrotaenia in a tropical rainforest terrarium.

cant in subtropical or mountainous areas. It is mandatory that you research the species you intend to keep if you are not yet familiar with its climatic requirements. AdCham.com maintains a database of chameleon species (*http://www.adcham.com*) with lots of valuable information.

In the forests south of the equator, temperatures are very stable and fluctuate little. In the tropical lowlands, temperatures drop by 8–10°F (4–5°C) at night, and by 15–20°F (8–10°C) in the mountains and desert areas. Most species of chameleons require these night drops to stay healthy. In any case, be sure to research the climatic conditions in which your species live.

Attention!

The temperatures in the previous tables represent the range of minimum and maximum day temperatures you can expose your animals to.

Sudanese

(*C. calcaricarens, C. calyptratus, C. namaquensis, C. zeylanicus*)

Sudanese and Sudano-Guinean enclosures are best made out of screened cages and illuminated by metal halides. Humidity is provided by a fogger for one hour in the early morning, and the chameleons have access to a drip system for their water requirements. To simulate the rainy period, a misting system can run for several minutes per day, on the condition that the air temperature does not exceed 78°F (26°C).

Forest Edge

(*Furcifer labordi, F. pardalis, C. gracilis, C. quilensis*)

Forest-edge terrariums are best made out of glass with an active evaporation system (forced-air convection). If the RH of the ambient air is already high, screened cages are an option. They can be illuminated with fluorescent lamps or metal halides. Misting to allow the animals to drink should be done manually.

Plateau

(*Furcifer campani, F. lateralis, F. minor*)

Preferably, plateau terrariums should consist of screened cages in a temperature-controlled room, but air-conditioned glass terrariums have given me very satisfactory results. Metal halide lighting is necessary to allow the animals to warm themselves to their preferred body temperature (PBT). Humidity is provided by a misting system to replicate the rainy season.

Equatorial Rainforest

(Chamaeleo cristatus, Chamaeleo quilensis, C. oweni)

Equatorial rainforest terrariums are best made out of glass and cooled with passive evaporation. They need moderate lighting, so fluorescent lamps are a good bet. The ambient RH and temperature need to stay stable throughout the year. A misting system with nozzles can be used for a few minutes during the cooler time of the day. Seasonal fluctuations of RH (high relative humidity—low relative humidity) over more or less extended times might be necessary to induce breeding. A small waterfall with a good filtering system at the back of the terrarium can be an interesting addition to help humidify and cool the setup.

Tropical Rainforest

(Calumma gastrotaenia, C. parsonii, Furcifer balteatus)

Tropical (Malagasy) rainforest enclosures are best built as screened enclosures; if they must be glassed in, good ventilation is essential. They need moderate lighting, so fluorescent bulbs are appropriate singly or paired with metal halides. A misting system is a necessary addition to the setup, but it should not be running if the ambient temperature is over 73°F (23°C).

Equatorial Afromontane

(Chamaeleo deremensis, Chamaeleo johnstoni, C. quadricornis, Kinyongia fisheri)

Afromontane chameleons need moderate to intense lighting, good

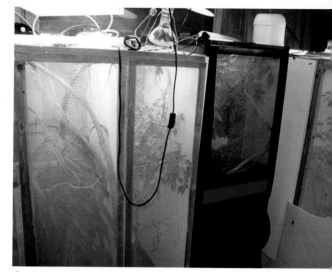

Some chameleons are very territorial. Visual barriers between cages are necessary to avoid stress. "Plateau species" are being kept in these cages.

airflow, and high humidity. Both screened cages and forced-air terrariums are appropriate for keeping these chameleons if fluorescent lighting is being used. If intense light is needed in the enclosure for sun-loving species, screened cages should be kept in a cool room and glass terrariums should be cooled with a miniature air-conditioning system. For Cameroon and East African species, a fogging system will be needed to replicate the high, cool humidity that comes with passing clouds. A misting apparatus should also be in place to simulate heavy rainfalls, but be sure to cool the ambient temperature to 68°F (20°C) and note that night temperatures can be even cooler, with a 100 percent RH created by the fogger.

Chapter Nine
Nutrition

Chameleons' food is chemical energy. A chameleon diet is sufficient if:

- it supplies the elements needed to produce energy (carbohydrates, fats).
- it supplies good-quality proteins to ensure growth and physical health.
- it contains micronutrients in adequate quantities: minerals (sodium, potassium, magnesium, calcium, iron, copper, zinc, manganese) and trace elements (iodine, selenium, sulfur).
- it is rich in vitamins and antioxidants (carotenoids, vitamins A, C, and E, natural oxidants found in food and plant material).
- it provides a healthy balance between bulk and nutritional value.
- it is nontoxic.

Best Live Feeder Insects

The best live feeder insects are gut-loaded, meaning that they have been fed a diet rich in specific elements, such as calcium and vitamins, that increases their nutritional value. The top three feeder insects for chameleons are crickets (nymph and adult, rich in fats and proteins, good chitin content), flies (adult, rich in vitamins and proteins, good chitin content, easy to digest), and silkworms (rich in calcium, proteins, and fiber, very easy to digest, but low in chitin content. However, even these staple feeding insects have some nutritional deficiencies. Because chameleons have very high requirements for various complex antioxidants, you will need to supplement their diets with a mineral/vitamin mix to avoid health problems.

Important Note

Crickets and several other insects (mealworms) have a poor calcium to phosphorus ratio, which must be improved (brought closer to 2:1). Feed your crickets a high-calcium diet (preferably a commercial cricket food) or sprinkle a good mineral/vitamin on the insects before feeding them to your chameleons.

Vitamins and Minerals

Calcium and phosphorus are minerals used by chameleons for proper bone construction. Calcium ions are also needed for proper muscle function.

Many mineral/vitamin mixes for chameleons are available. The best ones include a large quantity of micronutrients (vitamins, minerals, trace elements), and are water soluble (they can be mixed with water and sprayed on chameleons to drink and also used in gut-loading flies). Most of the time, instructions for these mixes require you to add them to the insect food or sprinkle them onto the insects right before offering them as food. In that case, products with good adherence are best, as powders tend to fall off the insects with time.

Water

Chameleons like to drink rainwater, or water droplets left on leaves by dew or rainfall. You can automatically administer water from sprinklers, or misting nozzles, or manually from a pipette or a vaporizer. The latter can be consuming if you have a lot of chameleons.

Important Note
You might want to add some powdered pollen and powdered astaxanthin (an algae grown commercially as shrimp feed available from *www.cyanotech.com*), or powdered cacti pads and hibiscus leaves (*www.carolinapetsupply. com*), to your mineral/vitamin mix for better results. Keep your mixtures in a dark, cool place.

Diets for Different Needs

Maintenance Needs
A maintenance diet is the quantity of nourishment a chameleon must have each day to maintain a constant weight and remain in good health. It does not take into consideration the extra nutrition needed for

Calumma parsonii parsonii *(female).*

reproduction, growth, or tissue repair (in case of a sick or injured animal). It can be evaluated empirically or calculated for veterinary or research purposes (to fatten up or slim down some animals), but usually, when the animals are given enough room to exercise and a diet that is both balanced and rich in nutrients, there is little need to worry and your animal should remain in good health.

Repair and Growth

A diet for repair and growth provides a normal quantity of food beyond maintenance needs. A repair and growth diet allows lizards to (re)construct their bones, muscles, and internal organs, while also building up reserves. For this reason, the emphasis should be put on protein, mineral, and trace element (in particular iodine) intake, rather than fat intake.

Cricket nymphs, gut-loaded flies, and silkworms can constitute the basis of the diet, but efforts should be made to provide greater dietary variety. Iodine is a critical trace element in the growth and health of baby chameleons. You can mix iodine-rich powdered sea kelp (kombu, available at *www.kassiba.com*) into drinking water and offer it to the flies, which are always thirsty.

Reptiles continue to grow throughout their lives. It is therefore essential to take into account growth and reproduction needs when feeding the animals under your care. Baby and young chameleons should be fed liberally to promote daily weight gain.

Reproduction

A month before chameleon mating is anticipated, the diet should consist mainly of crickets and flies gut-loaded with carotenoids (astaxanthin, alpha and beta carotene, lutein, lycopene) from fresh vegetables, flowers, and fruits, as well as vitamin E (corn, pollen). Adding a vitamin/mineral/trace elements mix to the insects is absolutely necessary to ensure nothing is missing from the diet. The animals should also be exposed to natural sunshine for vitamin D_3 photosynthesis and stimulation of the parietal eye.

Egg Production

Egg production requires nourishment above and beyond a female's maintenance rations. These nutritional requirements increase with gestation as well.

Egg formation in the female's body consumes a great deal of energy and a great many food elements. As the eggs grow, they become heavier and take up more and more room in the body cavity, sometimes as much as 50 percent of the female's weight and up to 80 percent of the space in the body cavity. Food bulk in relation to its nutritive value has to be reduced. Insects high in chitin (giant mealworms, beetles) must be avoided, whereas gut-loaded flies (proteins, carbohydrates, iodine, powdered milk, and supplement mix), silkworms, and waxworms and adult crickets are preferred.

Brumation

When preparing for brumation, a dormant period during which food intake and physical activity are diminished, animals should be fattened up so that they can tap into their reserves during the weeks of cold torpor. A diet a bit richer in giant mealworms, hissing cockroaches, and waxworms is appropriate. Once the animals have gained fat reserves, which can be seen in their well-rounded tails and beefy cheeks, they can be put into "slow-mo" mode, with diminished temperature, light, RH, activity, and food. They should always be offered drinking water laced with nutritional supplements with a pipette or a syringe (without the needle) and fed a maintenance diet.

Chamaeleonids living in tropical and subtropical areas go into slow-motion mode for a couple of months during the winter. During this period, their food intake is reduced but not stopped. For semi-hibernating chameleons, such as some tropical mountain species like *Rhampholeon acuminatus, Rh. viridis*, Carpet chameleon (*Furcifer lateralis*), South African dwarves (*Bradypodion* sp.), and the common chameleon, food

Chamaeleo jacksonii xantholophus *resting.*

intake can be nonexistent for as long as the cold period lasts.

During aestivation, a period of summer dormancy that occurs in tropical species living in deciduous forests, many chamaeleonids will take refuge underground and will considerably slow their metabolism. During this time, the animals do not eat or drink. This period can last for several months in western Madagascar.

Chapter Ten

Raising Insects

Should you breed your own insects? If you have a large chameleon collection, if you are a professional breeder, or even if you are a small, private breeder, you might want to consider this option. Breeding and raising your own chameleon food source will be a bit of extra work—and it is a good idea to have a separate space to do this— but it will give you better control over the food you give your animals. In any case, the information presented here is always handy to have.

Crickets

Acheta domestica

The house cricket (*Acheta domestica*) is the chameleon's favorite crick. Its cousins, *Gryllus bimaculatus* and *G. campestris*, are larger and dark brown and emit

Attention!

All non-native herbivorous insects (such as roaches) require a federal permit from the USDA. They are widely sold without, but technically a permit is required.

strong odors that are off-putting to the animals. Many species of native crickets can be easily collected and are readily accepted by chameleons.

Why Crickets?

Crickets were the first successful feeder insects for chameleons. They are readily available pretty much everywhere nowadays, and they are easy to breed, feed, gut-load, and use.

Where to get crickets: You can obtain them from private and commercial dealers, pet shops, entomological supply stores, and universities.

Conditions required to keep them: Room temperature to low 90s (~32°C), 50% to 75% RH

How to Keep Them

Crickets' requirements for breeding are simple: They need warmth, food, water, a place to hide, and a place to lay their eggs. Any reasonably sized box will do if you intend to keep crickets, but be aware of the droppings they produce and the fact that good hygiene is mandatory to avoid strong odors. Crickets will feed on dry food (see next section), which can be offered to them on a plate. They can get water from fresh leaves of lettuce, or from a water dish with small pebbles in it on which they can climb and avoid drowning. The water will need to be replaced regularly and the pebbles cleansed. Commercial cricket-watering gel cubes (wet polyacrylate crystals) are another option.

Crickets are light-sensitive, and might shy away from strong light. They are also sensitive to condensation, mold, and bacteria, so adequate ventilation is essential. They will do better if given places to stand and hide, such as egg cartons, which can be stacked on top of each other and disposed of once they are sullied. Crickets lay their eggs in wet soil, but the soil must be replaced for hygienic purposes, with moist chunks of polyurethane floral foam (available from florists). Cricket eggs should be removed on a regular basis and left to hatch in their own boxes. Baby crickets are fed the same food as their parents.

Crickets.

Crickets are cannibalistic and will eat their own young anytime.

How to gut-load them: Crickets can be fed a dry mix of dog food, cat food, fish food, bird food, and goat pellets in equal parts. Water can be given to them in the form of fresh vegetables (lettuce) and chunks of orange. Boiled carrots, pumpkin, corn, and egg yolk can help to raise the carotenoid contents of the crickets when needed (when preparing chameleons for the breeding season).

Offering Crickets as Food

Sprinkle the crickets with a multivitamin/mineral/trace element mix on a daily basis, as crickets will lose some of their coating as they crawl around or groom themselves, and bring them to your chameleons. Some keepers leave their crickets in bowls or baskets, whereas others (like me) just leave them on egg cartons for the chameleons to come and eat.

Locusts

Locusta migratoria,
Schistocerca gregaria

Why Locusts?

Locusts are grass-eating insects and a good source of calcium for some species of chameleons.

Where to get locusts: During the summertime, if you have the opportunity to collect wild locusts and grasshoppers with a net in pesticide-free meadows, you should go for it. It's good exercise for you, and the results are even better for your chameleons. If you are looking into

breeding your own locusts, you can get starter insects or eggs from private breeders, entomological clubs and suppliers, local universities, etc.

Conditions required to keep them: Room temperature to low 90s (~32°C), 50% to 75% RH.

How to Keep Them

Locusts need to be caged in metal wire setups, as they will eat through plastic wire. The cages usually contain a jar of water in which fresh-cut wheat sprouts are left for the locusts to devour, a climbing area (metal mesh or similar), and an incandescent bulb as a heat source. Raising locusts is easy but not very convenient because of the odors generated without regular cleaning. Locusts reproduce easily and will lay their eggs (ootheca) in humid sand. For this reason, reproducing adults need pots of sand in their cages, into which females can lay their eggs. The eggs of some populations must go through a one- to three-month cooling period at 65°F (10°C) before being incubated at 90°F (32°C) for up to 20 days. The cooling period is critical for hatching success. A clutch generally has from 30 to 50 eggs. Eggs that do not require a diapause take two to three weeks to hatch at 90°F (32°C). Upon hatching, the young, which grow rapidly, should be placed in a similar screened cage. Young *L. migratoria* are orange and black; those of *S. gregaria* are yellowish, pink, and black. Both may be fed grassy wheat sprouts and oat or bran flakes. Locusts make excellent food for chameleons. They are rich in calcium and vitamins E and D. *S. gregaria* might be preferable because it feeds eagerly on cabbage, which is a good source of vitamin C, calcium, magnesium and iodine.

Offering Locusts as Food

Locusts are a great treat for chameleons, but the sharp rear legs with the thorny spurs should be removed beforehand to avoid injury to your animals.

Silkworms

Bombyx morii

Why Silkworms?

Silkworms have very soft skins; they are very nutritious, nutritionally balanced, and high in calcium. They also provide some roughage material (cellulose) to the chameleons.

Darkling beetle.

Conditions required to keep them: Room temperature to low 80s (~27°C), 75% RH.

Where to get silkworms: Silkworms can be purchased as eggs or larvae from distributors, along with the commercial food they need. Or, if you are fortunate enough to have your own mulberry plants, you might consider raising worms on your own plants, as it will be less time consuming. Remember that once silkworms have started to feed on fresh leaves, there will be no going back to artificial food.

Attention!

Because silkworms eat constantly in a stationary mode, they produce a lot of feces, which, if eaten by mistake, can kill them. They also have particular RH requirements, and desiccate easily. Consider these issues seriously if you are living in a dry area and do not want to lose your worms.

How to Keep Them

Silkworms can be started with artificial food that you prepare for them and store in the refrigerator (or deep-freeze) when it is not being used. It is important to offer the food at room temperature. If you have a lot of chameleons, a simpler way to go is to grow your own mulberry trees, as the artificial food is rather expensive, and silkworms eat a lot and make a mess.

Offering Silkworms as Food

Either hand silkworms directly to your animals, or pick up the silkworms on their cubes of food and place them in the enclosure for your chameleons to come and eat.

Flies

Musca domestica

Why Flies?

Flies are readily accepted by all chameleons. They come in all kinds and sizes, and maggots are inexpensive, easily metamorphosed, and gut-loaded.

Conditions required to keep them: Room temperature to mid-80s (~27°C), 50% to 75% RH.

Where to get flies: Fishing stores and pet shops, or start a breeding colony by yourself.

How to Keep Them

Keep the maggots in sawdust, in a shady, well-ventilated place from 72–82°F (22–28°C). As the maggots pupate, they will turn brown to

Attention!

You might want to avoid catching your own flies for health reasons. Even if the risk is limited for chameleons whose immune system can handle bad strains of *E. coli*, it's best to get maggots that have been raised on tofu or soybean meals, so that you don't carry the risk transmitting nasty bacteria to your animals.

black. If you want to retard the metamorphosis of some of the pupae into flies, leave them at 50°F (10°C). Remove the pupae as you need them and place them at the bottom of an open jar. Cover the jar's opening with nylon pantyhose and tie the ends around its neck. At 80–90°F (27–32°C), the pupae should emerge a few hours later.

How to gut-load them: Flies are always thirsty and always looking for sugar, so the best way to prepare a fly gut-load mix is to mix some sugar with water, powdered milk, pollen,

Hydei fruit flies.

multivitamins, minerals and trace elements.

Offering Flies as Food

Once gut-loaded, the flies can be released in the chameleons' enclosures. Cultures of flightless houseflies are available from biological supply stores.

Giant Mealworms

Zoophobas morio

Why Giant Mealworms?

Large chameleons readily accept giant mealworms, which are more nutritious and less fattening than the smaller mealworms (*Tenebrio molitor*).

Conditions required to keep them: Room temperature to low 80s (~27°C), 50% to 75% RH.

Where to get giant mealworms: They are widely available from live-food dealers and professional breeders, pet shops, etc.

How to Keep Them

These larvae are easily raised in a terrarium or in a tub containing bran mixed with powdered wheat germ, brewer's yeast, pieces of carrot, and chopped fruits. Larvae need to be kept singly in a moist medium (peat

Find Out More on the Web

www.shopspiderpharm.com/ servlet/Detail?no=26

moss, for example) to pupate and mature. The adults can be kept on the bran/wheat germ medium to lay their eggs and complete the cycle.

Offering Giant Mealworms as Food

Since these insects tend to crawl, it is best to either offer them from your hand to your animals or to put them in a bowl where they can be picked up by the chameleons. These grubs are best offered as treats or supplements and should not be part of the staple diet of your animals, as they are very fattening.

Hissing Cockroaches

Gromphadorhina portentosa

Why Hissing Cockroaches?

If you intend to keep large species of chameleons, such as *Chamaeleo melleri, F. oustaleti,* and *C. parsonii,* hissing cockroaches are a great treat item and should be part of their weekly diet.

Conditions required to keep them: Room temperature to low 90s (~32°C), 50% to 75% RH. (Within these parameters, as with all roach species, there will be a great variation in growth rate and reproduction.)

Where to get hissing cockroaches: Specialized labs, breeders, and some pet shops might be able to help you with a starter colony of hissing cockroaches.

How to Keep Them
Hissing cockroaches can be kept in boxes or terrariums filled on the bottom with moist cocoa shell mulch. These insects feed on carrots, apples, dry dog food, and oranges. Care should be taken to avoid food from spoiling and attracting ants.

Madagascar hissing cockroach.

Offering Hissing Coackroaches as Food
They can be directly offered to chameleons as treats or left in plain view for the animals to take a shot at them.

Waxworms
Galleria mellonela

Why Waxworms?
Waxworms are an enery-rich food, best used sparingly on chameleons, or as an addition to their diet to fatten them up before brumation.

Conditions required to keep them: Room temperature to low 80s (~27°C), 75% to 80% RH.

Where to get waxworms: Purchase them from beekeepers (for whom they are a pest), from fish stores (where they are sold as bait), live-food dealers, and pet shops.

How to Keep Them
These caterpillars can be safely refrigerated when not in use. Otherwise, you will need a large plastic bucket with some food and larvae. Ventilation is provided by a hole in the lid, which is covered with metallic mesh. You can raise waxworms on a paste made of
- 6 ounces (175 g) honey
- 2.7 ounces (75 g) powdered wheat germ
- 6 ounces (175 g) glycerin
- 3.7 ounces (75 g) yeast
- 17.6 ounces (500 g) corn flour
- 17.6 ounces (500 g) pollen

Place the paste in the bucket, along with some adult moths. The females will quickly lay their eggs on the paste, they will hatch in 14 days at 84°F (29°C). The worms will start tunnelling in the food (hence their scientific name), which are easy to pull apart when you need to remove the caterpillars.

Superworm, **Zophobas morio.**

Offering Waxworms as Food

Give waxworms as an occasional treat, help fatten up skinny animals. Waxworms are not easily digested by chameleons.

Fruit Flies

Drosophila funebris, Drosophila melanoleuca

Why Fruit Flies?

Fruit flies are a good food for hatching chameleons and for the smallest species (stump-tailed chameleons, *C. nasuta, K. oxynorhinum*).

Conditions required to keep them: Room temperature to mid-70s (~22°C), 50% to 75% RH.

Where to get fruit flies: You can obtain them from commercial dealers, entomological suppliers, and universities.

How to Keep Them

Keep fruit fly cultures preferably in glass jars, under 12 hours of light per day. You may prepare your own culture medium for fruit flies if none is available commerically to you. Take 2.65 ounces (75 g) of agar, and 5.30 ounces (150 g) of yeast (*Saccharomyces cerevisiae*, or "beer yeast"), and dissolve and boil in 1.16 gallons (4.4 l) of water. Add 1.65 pounds (750 g) of maize meal, 2.82 ounces (80 g) of soy meal (optional, can be replaced with maize meal), 13.50 fluid ounces (400 ml) molasses, and 27 fluid ounces (800 ml) malt syrup. Dissolve and boil again, stirring constantly. Let the mixture cool down to 140–160°F (70–60°C). Then add and stir in 0.68 fluid ounces (20 ml) propionic acid (100% concentration) and 1.70 fluid ounces (50 ml) of Nipagin (8% concentration).

The culture medium is then transferred to glass jars and some moistened yeast pellets (human grade, available at supermarkets) can be added to the surface of the medium for the fruit flies to feed on. Paper towels can be used to remove extra water; if the mixture is too loose, the flies might drown or not lay any eggs. Change and clean the bottles on a regular basis to ensure that the flies are not parasitized by mites.

Offering Fruit Flies as Food

Fruit flies need to be enriched with a vitamin/mineral mix. They can then be fed to the chameleons.

Chapter Eleven

Inducing Reproduction in Captive Chameleons

Chamaeleonids will reproduce easily under proper human care when their needs are met. Understanding, and, whenever possible, re-creating the climatic conditions of the chameleon's natural habitat are essential, because it is they that trigger sexual activity. For breeding purposes, you may wish to have a particular setup to cycle your animals and possibly an outdoor enclosure to expose them to beneficial sunlight.

For chameleons in the wild, reproductive functions peak shortly after periods of prolonged cooler weather, social isolation, or dormancy. Alternatively, they may be triggered by a change in food, hormonal and endocrinal factors, relative humidity, rainfall, photoperiod, temperature, or a combination of all of these.

Clutches and viable hatchings are linked to the nutritional intake of the females. Food supplemented with vitamin E, provitamin A or carotenoids, iodine, calcium, and proteins is essential to successful reproduction of the animals. Deficiencies in these elements have been linked to low clutch yields, infertility, stillbirth, late hatching, and baby deaths in chameleons.

In male chameleons, obesity and stress due to peer pressure have been linked to infertility and loss of libido. It is important that the males are lean, which should be a given after a dormancy period, and psychologically healthy.

Breeding Cycles

In species that experience a dormant period (the typical chameleon, and Malagasy, tropical montane, and subtropical species), the concentration of the sex hormones (testosterone and estradiol) in the blood elevates for several weeks after their emergence from brumation. The heightened levels of these hormones correspond with the expected vitellogenic and ovulatory cycles in females, and with the onset of active sperm production in males. Under human care, these species need the same type of rest. In the wild, brumation lasts for six to ten weeks in species experiencing a

The hemipenis can be seen in this photo.

cool-down in their humid environment (low 70s°F [low 20s°C], RH around 75 percent). Aestivation lasts for five to seven months for species hiding under dead leaves or in crevices in deciduous forests to escape from the drought and the cool (low 70s°F [20s°C] RH around 35 percent), and then from the drought and the heat (high 70s°F [high 20s°C]), such as is the case for *Furcifer lateralis* and *Brookesia decaryi*. In captivity, however, such lengthy periods of dormancy are neither necessary nor desirable; 45 to 90 days is sufficient for most species.

Other tropical species will be ready to mate as soon as they have reached adulthood and have consumed enough food to ensure egg production. In captivity, *Furcifer minor* take about seven to eight months to reach sexual maturity. Females that have been fed liberally grow with fully formed egg follicles and are ready to breed with any mate. Females that have been fed on a more restrictive diet will delay follicle and egg production until enough food is available, an event that has been observed by other authors. One Dutch breeder published his observations on female *Furcifer pardalis*, remarking that their receptiveness to mating could be assessed by the length of their nails (long nails = sexual receptiveness), as nails are used to dig burrows for egg nests in the soil.

Parson's chameleons court and need space.

In equatorial species, breeding usually takes place after the animals have been able to store enough nutrients during a period of slower activity, which usually corresponds to the most favorable time for feeder insects. Breeding occurs after the cloudy, slightly cooler weather and higher humidity of the monsoon (low to mid-70s°F [low to mid-20s°C], RH up to 100 percent), have passed and sunny days are back. Sun seems to play an important role in male sexual aggressiveness in some species of *Kinyongia* and *Cham-aeleo* alike (*K. oxynorhina*, *K. xenorhina*, *C. johnstoni*).

It is therefore important not only to cycle the animals in view of their reproduction, but also keep in mind that the amount of food they receive will trigger egg production, which is demanding on the females' health and life spans.

Breeding Techniques

To breed chameleons, you must have at least a pair of compatible adult chameleons. Three types of

Kinyongia tavetana

breeding systems can be used singly or in combination with each other: harem mating, pair mating, and time mating.

Harem Mating

Harem mating involves providing several females for one male, or vice-versa. Chameleons are kept in groups and are free to choose their own mate. It is recommended for slow-growing species living in spacious enclosures or free-range rooms, as these animals might engage in lengthy courtships (*Calumma parsonii* and *C. melleri*, for example). At times, male rivalry is necessary to provoke the animals and initiate active courtship. If this is the case, you might make use of a mirror so that the males can see their reflections from time to time. This will give them excitement and the stimulation they need to mate without getting hurt.

Pair Mating

In pair mating, a chameleon is kept together until copulation has taken place. It is indicated for "aggressive" heliophilic (sun-loving) species that do not engage in lengthy mating rituals, such as *Chamaeleo calyptratus* and *Furcifer* species. These types of chameleons are stimulated by sunlight, so make sure to breed them on a warm, sunny day, or under strong lighting.

Calumma gastrotaenia *mating occurs after a resting period.*

Gravid female **Furcifer balteatus** *showing a pink coloration.*

Multiple Mating

Multiple mating has been observed in several species of *Chamaeleo* (*C. deremensis, C. jacksonii*) and *Bradypodion*. Receptive females will mate with more than one male over a period of a few days or longer in the case of *C. deremensis*. Multiple mating can be attempted as long as females are receptive, and it may ensure a clutch with genes from different males.

Caring for Gravid Females

As soon as mating has occurred, females go through a hormonal change that becomes obvious within minutes as their coloration and temperament change. Many females become hostile to males of their own species, and it is best to give them a place of their own. During and after this period of time, they should be fed a regimen of higher-quality food (silkworms, gut-loaded flies supplemented with multivitamins, powdered sea kelp—kombu and nigari water in small doses also do wonders—minerals, and trace elements) rather than crickets alone.

The enclosures should be prepared according to the factors gravid females are known to look for, such as the soil's physical feel and composition (dead leaves, humus, or sandy) warmth, and possible nesting sites (mounds of dirt facing the morning sun, plant roots in a pot, shade).

It is usually necessary to separate the male and female after copulation, as both sexes can be aggressive toward one another.

Time Mating

Time mating involves breaking an isolation and/or resting period by introducing a sexual partner into the territory of a potential mate. I recommend it for species with a softer temperament, but also for species experiencing little climatic variation in their natural habitats, such as *Chamaeleo jacksonii, Chamaeleo quadricornis, Chamaeleo johnstoni,* and *C. malthe*. For example, you might switch on the lights of your enclosure and introduce a male to a female in the middle of the night, or leave a female in the enclosure of an isolated potential mate.

Some breeders create a hot spot under a barren area in the enclosure where the female can lay her eggs, whereas others prefer to move their gravid females to new setups. Some even put them inside large buckets filled with nothing but 12 inches of substrate, which is probably a bit stressful for the animals. The egg-laying operation should be monitored and the eggs removed from the nesting site as soon as the female is finished with her work.

Dystocia (Difficult Oviposition)

Egg-bound females can also be offered a few drops of calcium lactate (in a concentration of 15 grams per liter) or calcium gluconate in similar proportions. If things do not get any better by the next day, a few drops of a mixture made out of water and Vaam powder (an amino acid mix used by athletes as a sports drink to enhance their endurance) has helped several of my egg-bound female chamaeleonids.

Proper Nutrition

Some females may be egg-bound or experience a difficult oviposition. The contraction of the muscles requires calcium ions to be transferred from the blood to the muscle cells. To avoid depleting the female's calcium reserves during the oviposition, proper nutrition before, during, and after this period is critical.

Furcifer oustaleti *laying her eggs.*

Peritonitis

In females, peritonitis (inflammation of the peritoneum, the abdominal cavity membrane) may result from a rupture of the oviducts or the eggs. Peritonitis can sometimes be identified by a bright yellowish spot

The yellow discoloration on the snout of this **Calumma cucullata** *(female) is an indication of palate abscess (mouth rot).*

Furcifer antimena digging to deposit her clutch.

on one of the animal's flanks (the infection causes discoloration of the chromatophores.) The condition is mostly observed in wild-caught animals, and it requires urgent medical assistance from a veterinarian, antibiotic treatment, and possible surgery.

Cloacal Prolapse

Cloacal prolapse is a medical condition by which the terminal section of a chameleon's intestines falls down and comes out of place through the cloaca. Prolapsed cloacae, both in male and female chamaeleonids, are best treated surgically by veterinarians.

Caring for Eggs

Removing Eggs from Nesting Sites

Once the female is done with oviposition, the eggs can be removed. This must always be done carefully. You might want to have your containers with the incubating substrate ready, so that you can move the eggs as rapidly as possible.

The species, date of oviposition, number of eggs, and expected hatching period should be indicated with a permanent marker on the container. The incubating temperature(s) should be decided beforehand and can be entered in a database for reference and to evaluate any temperature during incubation.

You will need to dig in the substrate to reach the eggs, but be sure you are doing it with care, particularly when the substrate is compact. Make sure your hands are clean, dry, and, most important, free of chemical substances. When removing eggs from their burrow, be sure to note their original position, possibly by putting a mark with a soft, nontoxic pencil on the top of each egg. They can then be inserted horizontally, half their width deep in the new substrate, at a slight distance from one another. Chameleon eggshells are naturally coated with an antibacterial substance meant to protect them from contamination. It is therefore important not to wash the eggs, even if you find dirt on them. Powder-free latex gloves will prevent skin oils from clogging the egg's air pores.

Find Out More on the Web
www.vaam-power.com/

Incubating Substrates

Many types of substrates can be used to incubate chameleon eggs, but whatever you use must be free of chemical additives. Substrates provide support to the eggs and prevent their desiccation. Eggs absorb the water from the substrate through infiltration.

I use four kinds of substrates in incubating containers: perlite, sphagnum, vermiculite, and volcanic soil. Incubating containers are clear small plastic containers with lids. Small aeration holes may or may not be drilled in their sides.

A clutch of incubating Chamaeleo wiedersheimi *eggs.*

Substrates can be dry or moist to the touch, but they should *not* be too fine or wet to the touch.

Perlite: Perlite should be used for eggs that need good substrate aeration and that would not do well getting direct contact with water or a damp substrate (*C. eisentrauti, C. johnstoni*). The eggs can be placed onto a one-inch layer of perlite and covered half to three-quarters to their tops. A funnel reaching to the bottom of the container is used to direct water to the lower part of the perlite. If the eggs need a cool incubation, 60s to low 70s°F (~16°C to ~22°C), you should direct the fog of a cool, ultrasonic humidifying machine inside the incubation chamber with the help of a plastic duct to raise the humidity to the desired level.

Sphagnum: Sphagnum can be used as an incubating medium for eggs with short incubation times at room temperature, such as eggs of stump-tailed chameleons. You should verify that the sphagnum is free of insects and invertebrates, as this substrate might not be sterile. Eggs can be deposited between two layers of sphagnum moss; water can be sprinkled over the top layer.

Volcanic soil: Although likely not sterile, volcanic soil is a great substrate for species that need good

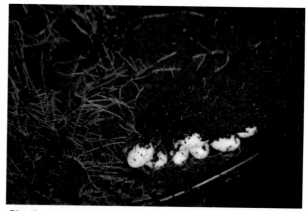

Plastic covering being torn apart to access the eggs.

Eggs of the Rhampholeon *species.*

**Find Out More
on the Web**
www.kassiba.com

aeration and a heightened substrate humidity and temperature to hatch (*F. labordi, F. lateralis*). Eggs should be buried halfway or up to two-thirds of their height in very slightly moist, not too fine (the eggs need oxygen) volcanic soil. In order to avoid touch-

ing the eggs, water can be added manually by means of a funnel reaching to the bottom of the substrate, added on the side, or set in small reservoirs inside the container with the eggs if the heat inside the incubator permits evaporation. Increases in water content should correlate with increases in temperature inside the incubator. Do not increase the water content of the substrate if the incubating temperature is on the cool side, for example, during the cold torpor or the diapause.

Vermiculite: Coarse vermiculite has been used successfully as a substrate for reptile eggs for decades. Eggs should be buried halfway in moist vermiculite. Mix one part weight for weight of vermiculite with one part water. The vermiculite should be moist to the touch but not dripping when pressed between your fingers. Be sure to use horticultural-grade vermiculite, with no chemicals added to it. Vermiculite can be used for most chameleon eggs and for species requiring constant incubating conditions for their eggs.

Incubators and Incubation Techniques

Incubators are meant to keep the eggs at the necessary temperature

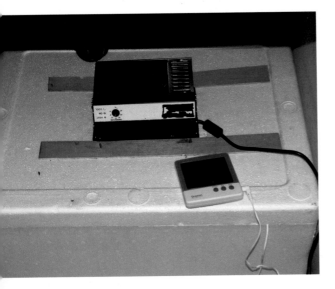

Cool incubator allowing for specific incubating temperatures.

for successful hatching. Techniques and equipment range from the very low-tech (boxes, vermiculite, and water left to incubate at room temperature) to the pretty elaborate (climate-controlled boxes), depending on the species and the breeder. Many eggs must go through cold diapauses, cool or warm torpors, and changes in RH before embryogenesis and hatching can begin.

The aquarium method for incubating eggs is usually not recommended, because the humidity cannot be properly regulated. Forced-air incubators with a temperature-control function are the best option for successful hatching. They should be well insulated and possibly have a window on the side, or movement sensors inside, to check on the incubating progress. Large Styrofoam boxes work well.

Inside the incubator, smaller containers half filled with substrate allow the eggs to develop until the incubation process is complete. As water evaporates, it raises the ambient RH in the incubator and simulates climatic change in the natural environment. In some cases, when a high RH is needed without high temperatures (*Chamaeleo eisentrauti*), it is preferable to use an ultrasonic humidifying system to raise the ambient humidity inside the incubating chamber.

Incubation Temperature

Only recently, it has been observed that egg incubating temperatures influence the sex of some

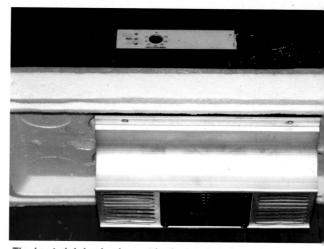

The heat sink (main element in the incubator) can be programmed to heat or to cool depending on the necessity.

species of chameleons. Temperatures on the cool side favor females, whereas temperatures on the hot side favor males. As a breeder, keep in mind that, although breeding a lot of females might produce a lot of eggs, males are responsible for gene pool diversity and vigor.

My experience with incubating temperatures is that, in the species I am working with, the low range of the incubation window produces females, whereas more males will hatch if the clutch is incubated on the higher side of the temperature range. Other breeders have experienced the exact opposite, with *C. chamaeleo chamaeleon*, for example, with low temps resulting in more males and high temps hatching more females.

When incubating chameleon eggs, you are always safer to stray on the slightly cooler side, at least in

Types of Incubation

Type	Example of Species
Sudanese	*C. calcaricarens, C. calyptratus, C. namaquensis, C. zeylanicus*
Sudano-Guinean	*Furcifer antimena, F. oustaleti, F. verrucosus*
Forest Edge	*Furcifer labordi, F. pardalis, C. gracilis, C. quilensis*
Plateau	*Furcifer campani, F. lateralis, F. minor*
Equatorial Rainforest	*Chamaeleo cristatus, Chamaeleo quilensis*
Tropical Rainforest	*Calumma gastrotaenia, Calumma parsonii, Furcifer balteatus, Furcifer minor*
Afromontane	*Chamaeleo deremensis, Chamaeleo johnstoni, C. quadricornis, Kinyongia fisheri*
Afro-Alpine	*Chamaeleo johnstoni, Kinyongia xenorhina, Rhampholeon acuminatus*

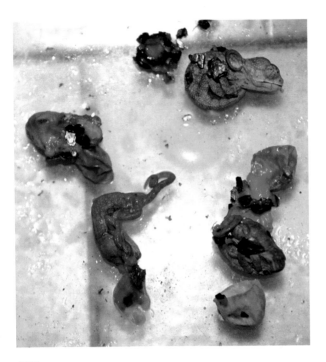

Stillborn babies due to a too high temperature at the end of incubation.

the first stages of incubation. By the end of the incubating period, babies benefit from a little boost in temperature and humidity to emerge from their eggs. If you are unsure about the humidity factor, remember that it works relative to the temperature, so when the temps go up or down, so should the humidity.

The table on page 103 illustrates temperature ranges for egg incubation. T° Timing indicates a temperature fluctuation for given periods of time (indicated in the cells as "mo" for months, i.e., 2 mo = two months, final = until hatching). Clutches of some species will not hatch without these temperature drops (particularly

Chamaeleonid Egg Incubation

Type	T° Timing	Night T°/Day T°	Notes and Comments
Sudanese	Unnecessary	78–82°F (26–28°C)	Start on slightly moist substrate, raise RH with T°
Sudano-Guinean	Unnecessary	77–80°F (25–27°C)	Start on slightly moist substrate, raise RH with T°
Forest Edge	Unnecessary	73–80°F (23–27°C)	Start on slightly moist substrate, raise RH with T°
Plateau	2 mo/2 mo/final	72–74°F (22–24°C)	57–63°F (14–17°C) 73–79°F (23–26°C)
Equatorial Rainforest	Unnecessary	73–79°F (23–26°C)	Constant RH
Tropical Rainforest	2 mo/10 mo/final	65–70°F (18–21°C)	72–74°F (22–24°C) 73–76°F (23–25°C)
Afromontane	Unnecessary	73°F (22.5°C)	Constant RH with constant T°
Afro-Alpine	Unnecessary	63–73°F (17–23°C)	Constant RH

F. campani, F. lateralis), whereas others will hatch at a constant temperature—for example, *F. minor,* at eight to nine months at 73°F (23°C), and occasionally *C. parsonii* at 74°F (24°C).

Some chamaeleon breeders induce a daytime/nighttime temperature to simulate the drop in temperatures. However, ten inches underground, these drops do not occur immediately, and the temperature fluctuates only by 2 to 4 degrees with the cooler or hotter seasons.

Excessive incubating temperatures are likely to kill the embryos or cause stillbirths. Eggs incubated at a slightly too-high temperature are also more likely to hatch weaker, smaller chameleons than if they had been incubated at lower temperatures.

Low temperatures should correlate with lower humidity, at least in the first stages of incubation. The length of the cold torpor should not be less than 45 days. Temperatures usually increase in slight increments, in correlation with the humidity. For more information on the species you are keeping, see species profiles in Chapter 14 and the incubation chart above.

Hatching of **Calumma parsonii.**

Egg Examination and Care

Eggs should be visually inspected on a regular basis, more frequently as hatching nears or when some change has occurred in the incubator, such as an increase in humidity or temperature. If everything seems to be

working well, I do not recommend candling the eggs, as this technique does not offer much information.

Expect the eggs to swell and enlarge as they incubate. By the end of the incubation period, some eggs might have quadrupled in size and weight. If you wish to take measurements of egg size and weight, remember to be careful when manipulating the eggs. Filled with liquid, they are also experiencing considerable inner tension, and might break more easily when touched.

Eggs with bright white shells are usually well calcified and should hatch properly. Poor calcification can be seen when eggs are yellowish in color and lacking firmness. These usually die well before hatching and rarely produce viable babies.

Problems and Remedies

Attacks on the eggs by small invertebrates in the container are very rare if sterile substrates have been used, but if they do happen, you need to move all the eggs to a new container.

Eggs might also be infertile and turn bad. All the eggs in a clutch might not be bad, but this is usually the case. All the bad eggs should be removed at once from the container and the good eggs left to incubate.

If eggs dehydrate during incubation (they show a dent or a depression on a large portion of their surface), it is necessary to moisten

C. labordi (male).

the substrate and use it to fully cover the eggs until they look well rounded again. A slight drop in incubating temperature can also help to avoid further dehydration.

If mold happens to grow on the eggs, sprinkle all of them with some athlete's foot powder medication at once.

Live Birth

Females from ovoviviparous, live-bearing, species of the genus *Bradypodion* and some of the East African subgenus *Trioceros* of *Chamaeleo* usually give birth in the morning, expulsing fully formed babies enclosed in a thin, transparent, sticky membrane through their cloacae. Air humidity is a key factor, as females will refrain from giving birth in a cage with a dry atmosphere (RH lower than 75 percent). In low humidity, the membranous sacs would quickly desiccate and imprison the babies as the female deposits them on branches and leaves.

Caring for Baby Chameleons

Once hatched, babies should be moved into small cages with other siblings. Some babies will hatch with their yolk sacs still visible. The yolk is a source of nutrition and water to the

Hatching of **Furcifer minor**. *Note the humidity on the substrate.*

babies, and it should be left alone until it has been absorbed, which takes about a day or two. Babies are kept at similar light levels as their parents, but at more moderate temperatures and at 80 percent air humidity. A good rule of thumb is to set an ambient temperature of no more than 74°F (23°C) with some

F. antimena *siblings exploring the ridge of their first cage.*

F. antimena *babies in a communal cage.*

hot spots where chameleons can bask, but be sure that the animals can't be burned.

A high RH of 75 to 85 percent is critical for babies, as they desiccate quickly; a low RH might claim the lives of your babies sooner than you could ever imagine. Once again, if in doubt, I recommend keeping your babies at an RH of no less than 75 percent and using a fogging system to create humid spots in the enclosures. Then let your animals decide for themselves and show you their preferences.

Houseflies make the best food for baby chameleons. They are readily accepted as food, chameleons digest them easily, and flies are easily gut-loaded with a mix of 1/3 mineral/vitamin mix, 1/3 glucose, and 1/3 powdered milk. Pinheads and ten-day old crickets are also good options for your baby chameleons. Aphids move too slowly to generate any interest in chameleons.

Water should also be offered on a daily basis, either pure or enriched with a vitamin/mineral mix, from a misting system.

Young animals have high food requirements and should be fed daily with vitamin/mineral-enriched insects. Babies should be kept by size, and the fastest-growing individuals should be removed and housed communally in larger cages as they grow.

Chapter Twelve

Health and Medical Aspects

Preventive Medicine

Common sense tells us that the best way to ward off diseases while keeping and breeding chameleons is to get only healthy specimens to begin with, and to keep them that way. Captive-bred animals, although they are not always parasite and disease-free, have a better chance at good health than wild-collected specimens. Lizards from the wild often arrive starved, physically injured, stressed, dehydrated, and parasitized. It is difficult to overcome these problems singly, and they are even more difficult to combat in combination.

Pathogens can be transmitted in various ways, by contagion (contact and airborne transmission), ingestion or inhalation (mycosis, eggs of parasitic worms), and blood parasites, which require a vector, usually a biting invertebrate (fly, mosquito, or mite), to be transmitted from one host to another. Of all the pathogens, the blood parasites have the easiest cycle to break, as it involves a vector

that has very little chance of survival outside the biome where the chameleons naturally occur. The simplest prophylactic measures include keeping your animals away from potentially infectious germ carriers (obviously sick and wild-caught specimens, dirty cages, equipment that has been used with sick or wild-caught animals), avoiding a high concentration of animals in cages (except if you are breeding them or keeping babies), and keeping their enclosures clean and at the desired conditions for the species.

Find Your Veterinarian

Finding a veterinarian is a critical step in maintaining your chameleon's health. The Association of Reptilian and Amphibian Veterinarians (ARAV) can help you locate the closest exotic DVM in your area.

Infectious Pathogens

Infectious diseases in chameleons have various origins, including

A pseudomonal infection (due to hot weather) and later gone systemic claimed the life of this hybrid chameleon of F. antimena *and* F. verrucosus.

viruses, bacteria, fungi, protozoa, and parasites.

Viruses

Viruses are elementary life-forms, visible only under electron microscopes. They are able to multiply only inside the living cells of their hosts, so no virus can be transmitted from the environment alone or from a dead chameleon. Viruses have been found in chameleons occasionally,

Avoid False Negatives

I suggest that serious hobbyists submit three fecal samples (so as to avoid false negatives) of their animals to their veterinarian for all newly acquired animals. This is especially important if they are to be introduced into a collection or mixed with other animals.

but they are not common and their effects are not known.

Bacteria

Bacteria are single-celled organisms without a nucleus, and they are found in different concentrations almost everywhere on earth. They multiply by fission and are classified according to shape:

- round   *Staphylococcus*
              Streptococcus
- curved   *Vibrio*
- spiral   *Spirochetes*
- straight   *Bacillus*

The pathogenic action of bacteria is due to secreted toxins (*Clostridium* sp.) and infections (tissue destruction) caused by multiplication (*Salmonella* sp.).

In chameleons, ubiquitous gram-negative, bacteria that do not retain crystal violet dye, anaerobic bacteria

are responsible for most bacterial infections, from mouth rot to pseudomonal skin infections. They appear most frequently in animals with depressed immune systems. Bacteria destroy good cells and produce toxins; they can even get into the bloodstream and reach other organs, including the brain. Prevention mainly consists of proper care and regular veterinary checkups.

Bacterial infections can be suspected when pus, skin discoloration, joint and eye inflammation, and unusual lethargic behavior are present. Infections are easily treated with electrolytes and broad antibiotic treatments (ceftazidime).

Fungi

Mold spores (*Fusarium* sp., *Paercilomyces* sp.) are widespread, and yeasts (*Candida albicans*) naturally occur in chameleons' intestinal flora. Infections usually affect the weakest chameleons' airways, joints, guts, and cloacal regions, as well as their skins. These microscopic fungi grow as colonies of single cells (in the case of yeasts) or as a multicellular network called a mycelium (molds). They produce chemicals called mycotoxins that destroy other cells and, ultimately, lead to total organ failure.

Diagnosis should be made after a culture has been confirmed from a swab. Fungi are numerous and live almost everywhere; however, they require a feeble immune system to take over a chameleon's health. Because they progress very slowly, the treatment is chronic.

Protozoa

Protozoans are single-celled primitive animals, and some species have a parasitic specialization. They use a host's cells, tissues, or blood to live and reproduce. In chameleons, we distinguish between blood protozoans and gastrointestinal protozoans. Blood protozoans in chameleons usually start and complete their life cycles in the blood of their host, but they need a biting or stinging invertebrate, such as a fly, tick, mite, or mosquito, as a carrier to transmit them to other hosts. These protozoans include *Plasmodium* sp. (responsible for malaria, they parasitize the red blood cells of chameleons), *Trypanosoma* sp. (the parasite responsible for sleeping sickness), *Leishmania* sp. (a parasite of the macrophages), and *Hepatozoon* sp., which lives in the blood.

Gastrointestinal protozoans live in chameleons' guts. They are usually ingested as oocysts, but sometimes as adults. Insects are often vectors, but they are not required for infection. Coccidian can be transmitted through sullied feeder insects or unhygienic conditions and biting might appear in captive-bred chameleons, whereas trypanosomiasis are very unlikely to be present in captive-bred animals as they require

A healthy Calumma cucullatus *(male).*

specific, wild, biting insects to transmit the parasite.

We can distinguish between amoebic illnesses (*Entamoeba invadens*), coccidiosis (*Isospora* sp., *Eimeria* sp.), and flagellate infections (*Trichomonas* sp.) because flagellate protozoa have little appendages that allow them to swim in their environment. These parasites are very detrimental to the health of chameleons, because they kill other cells, ulcerate epithelial cells in the gut, disturb normal gastrointestinal functions, and can lead to abscesses. Infected animals appear sick; they lose weight, experience stunted growth, and lose electrolytes with diarrhea. Preventive measures should include strict quarantine of infected animals. The addition of probiotics in the food is also highly recommended.

Endoparasites

Endoparasites are parasites found inside the chameleons. Subcutaneous parasites, like filarid worms under the skin, or internal parasites, like roundworms and blood parasites, can be found in wild-caught chameleons. The most obvious and common of these parasites are called microfilaria. Filaria are long, worm-like, smooth, white to bright-yellow roundworms classified as Nemathelminthes.

Nemathelminthes: Ascarids and filarids, also called nematodes, are migrating worms that move from one organ to another in the body of the animals. They are among the most common endoparasites found in chameleons and pass through the visceral organs, the digestive tract, or the lungs. Transmission occurs in two ways:

- Through the digestive tract by the ingesting of eggs or larvae, which then pass from the intestine to the bloodstream, creating tiny holes in the intestine. They eventually end their journey in the various organs of the chameleon. The eggs of these worms are expectorated or excreted by the infested host.
- Through stinging insects such as mosquitoes or ticks. These blood-sucking parasites play the role of carrier, passing microfilarids into the blood of the animals they prey upon. With time they mature and proceed to move about the host by

Closed eyes and prostration are associated with illness in chameleons.

perforating the tissues and the viscera. They end their cycle by forming a cyst in a specific organ (e.g., the lungs for *Rhabdias gemellipara,* the stomach for *Physalopteroides chameleonis,* the intestines for *Hexametra angustaecoides*, or the subcutaneous tissues for *Foleyella furcata*). The activity of these parasites creates lesions, which in turn cause obstructions and hemorrhages and result in secondary infections in the damaged organs, such as peritonitis or inflammation of the bronchial tubes.

With a microscope, microfilarids and filaria can be seen in a drop of blood or stools from infected wild chameleons.

Platyhelminthes (tapeworms): Tapeworms (cestodes) and non-annulated flatworms (taenias) are found in smaller numbers than nematodes in chameleons. The eggs of these worms are usually ingested when the mouths or tongues of the chameleons come in contact with infected soils. These worms take refuge in numerous organs, notably the heart and the circulatory system. Prophylactic measures are the same as those for gastrointestinal infections.

Trematodes (flukes): These flattened, non-annulated endoparasites are most commonly found in herbivorous lizards and tortoises. In chamaeleonids, flukes occur in the liver, pancreas, bile ducts, and intestine, from the stomach opening to the cloaca. How chameleons develop trematode infestations isn't really known. The lizards may swallow larvae clustered on grasses in humid zones or consume snails that carry the parasites. The pathological action of these parasites on chamaeleonids is also not very well known, but they might lead to secondary infections of organs, internal bleeding, and bacterial infections. Since the chameleon is the final host, the parasitic larvae mature and reproduce, and their eggs are then excreted by the chameleon.

Pentastomes (Throat and Lung Parasites)

Also called linguatids, pentastomes are a pararthopods—a group related to mites and ticks. They are found in most species of tropical lizards and in many other animals such as birds, snakes, and mammals. Their biological cycle and mode of transmission involve an intermediate herbivorous host, such as a locust or a grasshopper, that picks up the pentastome's egg with its food. The larvae develop in the primary host, which is then caught and consumed by the final host. In chamaeleonids, the larvae migrate to the respiratory system and settle in the trachea, alveoli, etc. An infected chameleon will cough up the newly laid eggs.

Pentastomes are whitish worms about 1 inch (2.5 cm) long. Prevention—by keeping infected specimens away from those that are not—is the best solution.

Ectoparasites

Ectoparasites are external parasites, mostly feeding on the blood of the animals they prey upon. They also serve as vectors for other blood parasites. Many of them are host/species-specific, and they attack by piercing or cutting through the skin with specialized jaw parts. Among others, they include there are acarian mites, ticks, mosquitoes, leeches, and flies. Acarian mites most plague baby chameleons and the Cameroon mountain chameleons. The ticks can be killed with specific products. For more information consult a veterinarian.

Other Illnesses

Immune System Diseases

Mountain and desert chameleon species require a significant night temperature drop to keep their immune systems in good condition. They also require healthy doses of

Attention!

In many cases, joint inflammations are due to bacterial infections, so a proper evaluation of the situation is advisable to avoid a misdiagnosis. Deformed jaws, soft bones, and twisted backs are generally related to metabolic bone disease (MBD).

antioxidants, which most species find in their food (carotenoids, vitamin E, and many others).

Gout

Gout is an inflammation of the joints of the legs and, at times, the backbone, caused by deposits of uric acid on cartilaginous parts. It is due to renal impairment, insufficient humidity, or lack of drinking water.

Metabolic pH Imbalances

Chameleons that have been exposed to high temperatures, been starved, been thirsty, or experienced diarrheic stools are likely to suffer from an electrolyte imbalance called metabolic acidosis. Metabolic acidosis can also be caused by an increase of carbon dioxide in the blood.

Metabolic alkalosis is typified by the loss of acids due to vomiting or following the administration of alkalizing salts. It may be triggered by an excess of calcium lactate if overdosed in gravid females or young animals.

Chameleons can be restored to health through oral or intravenous administration of salt solutions such as Pedialyte for a couple of days. It is advisable not to offer any vitamin/mineral mix before the proper PH balance has been restored.

Mineral and Vitamin Deficiencies

A bad diet will lead to mineral and vitamin deficiencies in chameleons. Over the long term, lack of proper

A sick **Chamaeleo johnstonii** *(female).*

proteins, calcium, or iodine might lead to rickets and dwarfed chameleons. In the short term, chameleons might cease to eat on their own if presented with the same deficient food, and in some cases, they may not be able to properly "shoot" their tongues at their prey (due to a calcium and vitamin B imbalance).

Various brands of vitamin and mineral mixes not only cover a very broad spectrum of deficiencies, but are also palatable and convenient to use on food insects. It is important that the calcium to phosphorus ratio in these commercial mixes is as close to 2:1 as possible. Both calcium and phosphorus are needed in equal parts for bone construction, but calcium is also required in other metabolic processes, including egg production and oviposition in females.

Extreme care is essential when handling small species such as Brookesia thieli.

Insects should also be gut-loaded with food including fresh vegetables and fruits before being offered to the animals. Wild-caught insects from meadows that have not been treated with pesticides can help to stimulate the feeding response in chamaeleonids. On a cautionary note, stinking insects, stinging insects, fireflies, and ants should be avoided.

Hunger strikes in chameleons might be an indication that something important is missing from their food. It is easily fixed by adequately enriching their diet with the micronutrients they need to maintain their health.

Common Ailments and Related Veterinary Medication

Symptoms of Bacterial Infections

Pneumonia: The animal has been exposed to cold temperatures and high humidity, it shows some breathing difficulty, and has mucous coming out of its gaping mouth.

Foot rot: The foot or the ankle is swollen; the swelling enlarges day after day.

Pseudomonal skin infection: Smallpox-like warts appear on the skin, usually during or after the animal has been exposed to high temperatures and high humidity.

Eye infection: A thick whitish material comes out of the eye, and there is swelling of the eye, which can remain closed for several days.

Amoebic gut infection: The animal displays sunken eyes and cheeks, running stools, apathy.

Stomatitis: Part of the jaw is swollen, the animal is reactive to the touch, and the skin might show some yellow discoloration on the swelling part. Upon internal inspection of the mouth, a variable quantity of a cheesy, yellowish mass is found.

Gut and Protozoan Infections

Coccidian: Fecal check
Amoeba: Fecal check
Helminthes: Fecal check

Medication and Antibiotics Used in Chameleons

Infection	Antibiotic	Administration
Respiratory	Ceftazidime, Ibilex syrup	DAILY × 1 for 10 days
Foot rot	Oxytetracyclin, injectable	Once every other day for 10 days
Pseudomonal skin infection	Surolan, Fucidin	DAILY, as long as necessary
Eye infection	Fucidin, Gentamicin, Chloramphenicol	DAILY × 2 for 5 days
Gut infection (bacterial)	Norflaxin	DAILY × 2 for 5 days
Stomatitis (Mouth rot)	Ibilex	DAILY × 1 for 7–10 days
Systemic infection-septicemia	Ceftazidime, injectable	Once every other day for 10 days
Coccidian infestation	Appertex	DAILY × 1 for 30 days
Protozoan gut infestation	Metronidazole	DAILY × 1 for 7 days/ 1 month later
Helmintic infestation	Febendazole	DAILY × 1 for 7 days/ 1 month
Fluke infestation	Spartrix	DAILY × 1 for 10 days
Microfilarid infestation	Ivermectin	1 time, renew 7 days later
Pentastomid infestation	Ivermectin	1 time, renew 7 days later

Flagellates: Fecal check
Flukes: Fecal check
Filarial: Probable in many wild-caught specimens of chamaeleonids
Pentastomids: Suspected when pneumonia is not an option

Medication posology depends on the animal. Consult with your veterinarian.

Medicines in chameleons work best when the animals are kept at their optimal metabolic temperatures, which vary according to species, and at times, individuals. It is also important to keep the animals in a stress-free enclosure or, for debilitated individuals, an incubator. It should also be noted that the basal metabolism of chamaeleonids is lesser than that of a warm-blooded animal. Therefore, the medications are broken down and filtered out twice as slowly as they would be in human beings. For this reason, precautions should be taken with antibiotics.

Clinical Procedures

How to Grasp and Hold a Chameleon

Grasping a chameleon by its nape, neck, spine, or tail will be interpreted by the animal as an aggressive gesture. Any forceful movement imposed too hastily or brutally on the animal will also be interpreted as a threatening gesture. It is best to slowly pick up the animal, or to encourage the chameleon to hold onto you. By placing your hand under its neck and belly, then slowly and gently raising your hand upward, you can usually induce it to step onto your hand. If an escape or fall seems imminent, gently enclose the chameleon with the other hand while allowing it to retain its grip. If absolutely necessary, immobilize it by enfolding its body gently into one hand and folding the forelimbs backward. Both hands and extra help might be needed to adequately restrain some large specimens.

How to Open a Chameleon's Mouth

Most of the time, gently rubbing the nose of a chameleon is enough to get it to open its mouth. If you don't get any reaction from this gesture, gently pinch the animal's lower lip as if to bring it forward, and the animal should soon open its mouth. With smaller chameleons (smaller species or babies alike), or very stubborn animals, it may be necessary to very carefully grasp the upper part of the throat and pull it downward. It is important that this be done very gently, as it can easily tear.

Chamaeleonids' teeth are brittle and easily broken if anything stronger

Holding a chameleon so as to get it to open its mouth.

than what they are used to forces its way in. Small injuries on the gums can lead to stomatitis and other problems.

Oral Administration of Food and Medicine

If the chameleon is able to eat, place the medicine in its mouth or mix it with some food, such as moist scrambled eggs which are always accepted by chameleons. If the animal refuses any kind of nourishment, slip a feline urinary catheter connected to syringe down its esophagus—be careful mind not to confuse it with the larynx overture, which is situated right behind the tongue and visible when chameleons breathe in or out—to administer food.

How to Give Injections to Chameleons

Subcutaneous injections can be given in the animal's flank. Gently pinch and lift up a bit of skin, then slip the needle quickly between the skin fold and the muscles. Great care must be taken when giving intramuscular injections. Insert the needle at a 45-degree angle, not too far into the femur muscle mass of the rear leg.

Slightly pinch and bring forward the lower lips.

Release the pressure applied by your fingers as the animal cooperates.

Calumma nasuta *(male)*.

Keeping the Chameleon's Mouth Open

Cut a small piece of semi-rigid plastic film, fold it in half, and drill a hole in the film that will allow you to observe the desired area of the mouth. Insert the folded film in the mouth of the chameleon, and unfold it while holding onto the head of the animal.

Diagnostic Aids

Visual Examination

Sometimes a visual physical examination of a chameleon can point to the source of the problem. Skin discoloration is generally present with bacterial infections. Dehy-drated, emaciated, lethargic animals can be suspected of coccidiosis. The filarids wild-caught chameleons harbor may be visible right under their skins.

Palpation

Examination by touch can allow clinicians or keepers to locate the painful area, or the reason for the animal's discomfort. Indeed, some chameleons can be felt "groaning" when touched on a sensitive area.

X-rays

X-rays can be used to diagnose osteodystrophy, kidney stones, skeletal deformities, encystments, or visceral lesions. Films currently available to radiologists provide excellent definition of both bone and soft tissues.

Blood and Fecal Tests

Blood tests can now be done with a single drop of blood to check on potential infections, parasites, and organ malfunctions. Fecal smears are useful to identify some parasitic infestations.

Autopsy

Autopsies can prove useful when the cause of death of a chameleon is unknown. For the most accurate results, take the chameleon to a specialized laboratory or veterinary clinic as soon as possible after death. The veterinarian must take into account all possible causal factors and potential illnesses; the animal's background information, origin of the specimen, age, feeding habits, general behavior, care, etc., is of great value to the diagnosis.

Anesthesia

To ease the pain of surgical procedures, suitable anesthetics must be used. Depending on the type and the extent of the operation, either a general or a local anesthetic will be required. To preclude anesthetic-induced problems, the safest and most suitable type for the intended procedure must always be sought.

Halothane (Fluothane, I.C.I), is the preferred anesthetic when general

This dissection of **Chamaeleo jacksonii xantholophus** *(female) shows the lungs, intestinal tract, and early eggs.*

anesthesia is required. It is an inhalent that must be administered very carefully in a special vaporizer or sealed box. A mixture of 3 percent pure oxygen for 15 ml of Halothane will put the animal to sleep quickly. Once anesthesia is induced, the amount of Halothane should be decreased to 1 percent in the same oxygen volume. This is sufficient to prolong sleep.

CAUTION!

Anesthetics should only be administered by veterinarians. The use of chloroform, ether, barbiturates, and many other sedatives can prove dangerous, if not deadly, to chameleons.

A Few Words on Chameleon Psychology

"This is anthropocentrism!" I can hear the indignant voices of some purist readers. Yet many of these people who have observed and kept these lizards for quite some time firmly believe that chameleons are probably the most sensitive members of the reptile kingdom.

Chameleons, like humans, are highly visual animals, so a lot of their intra-specific communication is done through body language, body positioning, and coloration.

Chameleons are very good at picking up fast movements. If coming from a small animal, they might elicit a hunting response, but coming from a larger animal such as a human, chameleons might get scared. It is always best to approach them and touch them slowly, at a chameleon pace.

Look into a chameleon's eyes when it is watching you. You will see fear, inquisitiveness, happiness, or whatever other emotion the animal is feeling reflected in its dilating and retracting pupils. Body language should also be studied.

Furcifer minor (*female*).

Interpreting Chameleons' Body Language

Mannerism	Meaning
Crawling in front of the glass of a terrarium	An expression of discomfort. The chameleon is stressed or unhappy. Lighting is insufficient, temperature is becoming too warm, or there are no climbing limbs.
Bobbing head	Claiming territory. Courtship behavior if vivid pattern is evident
Gaping mouth	Aggression
Gaping mouth with dark coloration and hissing	Extreme anger after being attacked or great fright
Gaping mouth with pale coloration	Overheated. Needs immediate cooling
Closing the eyes for abnormally long periods, even under normal conditions	Illness
Closing the eyes and hiding from another chameleon	Sign of being frightened by/of a cagemate
Vivid coloration with/without dark spots	Contentment/excitement
Vivid coloration with dark spots, gaping, and tail lashing	Anger
Pale coloration, chin and jaw idly resting on branch, tail coiled	Sleep position. Sign of relaxation
Vivid coloration with bright but sunken eyes	Thirst. (Dehydration can be determined by gently pinching the belly skin. Under normal conditions the skin should be supple and the pinched area should not remain visible.)
Dark coloration with submissive behavior; sleep posture when lying in the palm of the hand	I want to be petted/I enjoy being petted.

Remember: Never pinch or grasp a chameleon by the neck or backbone. Chameleons interpret this as a very threatening gesture.

Chapter Thirteen
Species Profiles

This chapter is meant as an overview of some interesting species, not an in-depth presentation. Please thoroughly research the species you intend to keep or are already keeping. In the descriptions that follow, I have used the term "Beginner" when I feel that the species is easily taken care of and would easily breed in captivity. "Intermediate" indicates a more demanding species.

Most of the true chameleon species mentioned in this chapter may be available as captive-bred specimens, usually from professional breeders and pet shops, and at times from occasional breeders and hobbyists. By supporting captive breeding operations, you play an active role in the preservation of your hobby, which should be a provider, rather than a mere consumer of chameleons.

When you join a chameleon keepers group, you will be able to share your enthusiasm and information with other breeders, and you may decide to join forces to breed other species of chameleons, support each other's breeding projects with breeding loans, or specialize in a particular species or morph of chameleons.

I personally recommend that any keeper or breeder invest in a small cooling system (available from *www.kassiba.com*) that may be used alternately for the incubation of the eggs, as a miniature air-conditioning system for small terrariums, or for the cooling of chameleons at nighttime. Another unit that will be very useful if you are keeping mountain chameleons is an ultrasonic humidifier. A lot of mountain chameleons need to breathe water droplets and will only stay healthy if this condition is replicated in captivity.

Find Out More on the Web
adcham.com/html/taxonomy/ species-taxonomy.html

C. parsonii *(male) orange eyes morph.*

Giant Parson's Chameleon

Calumma parsonii, Cuvier, 1824: Intermediate

Natural Distribution and Habitat

Distribution: Eastern coastal forests and mid-elevation rainforests, coffee plantations, forest edges, and degraded primary forests.

Climate preference: Tropical rainforest, 74–82°F (24–28°C) 75% RH.

Forest stratum: 6 feet up.

Breeding Data

Number of eggs per clutch: 20 to 40 eggs.

Number of clutches per year: One.

Hatching time: 18 to 21 months at fluctuating incubation temperatures, starting with a cold period of one month, with a minimum of 63°F and maximum of 77°F (17–25°C).

C. parsoni *(male) yellow lipped morph.*

C. parsoni cristiferi *(male) yellow morph.*

Sexual maturity: 20 to 24 months in captivity.
Life span: Over 10 years in captivity.
Maximum size: Males 32 inches (80 cm), females 30 inches (75 cm).

Terrarium Care
Terrarium type: Tropical rainforest.
Notes: The largest chamaeleonids on earth, Parson's chameleons are iconic figures for reptile enthusiasts. They are slow-moving, placid chameleons that shy away from frequent disturbance, and they would rather be observed than handled. Parson's chameleons naturally occur all along the east-coast rainforests of Madagascar, from the south to the north. At this time, four types are known: the "Orange-eyed," the "Yellow-lipped," the "Giant Yellow," and the smaller (15 inches [37 cm]) *C. parsonii* var. *cristifer,* which might well be a hybrid of *C. parsonii* and *C. globifer* since the two species are sympatric (two species with a different number of chromosomes that can breed and may have viable offspring) in their habitat, Madagascar's Andasibe nation park.

Parson's are slow-growing chameleons, and take more than a couple years in captivity to reach sexual maturity. During the first five months of life, they grow at a remarkably slow rate in comparison to other chameleons, before speeding up in their growth. For this reason, their food should be supplemented every other day rather than every day. The breeding success of this species is becoming more frequent. The females stay gravid for around four to five months, but the babies are seldom made available to the average keeper at this time.

In fact, these chameleons are not very difficult to breed. They fare better if left in large enclosures where they can be observed roaming around in pursuit of their daily activities.

Veiled Chameleon

Chamaeleo calyptratus, Dumeril, 1851: Beginner

Natural Distribution and Habitat
Distribution: High plateau and grasslands of Yemen, southwest Saudi Arabia.

Climate preference: Sudanese, Sudano-Guinean, Forest edge, plateau.
Forest stratum: Bushes, shrubs, eucalyptus trees, cultivated zones.

Breeding Data
Number of eggs per clutch: 30 to 70 eggs.
Number of clutches per year: Several.
Hatching time: 6 to 8 months at 80°F (27°C). Other breeders (Neãas, a renowned Czech chameleon specialist) recommend a daytime temperature of 86°F with a drop to 68°F nighttime (30°C daytime/20°C nighttime) until hatching (a bit less than 7 months).
Sexual maturity: 6 months.
Life span: 5 years.
Maximum size: Males 20 inches (50 cm), females 12 inches (30 cm).

Terrarium Care
Terrarium type: Sudanese, Sudano-Guinean, Forest edge, plateau.
Notes: The Veiled chameleon is a large, hardy, and very popular chameleon among enthusiasts, but it is rather aggressive. If males are housed with a harem of females, they remain very territorial and hostile to potential rivals, and even to their keepers if not handled regularly.

The Veiled chameleons are known for their eclectic food intake. In the wild, during the dry season, this species eats the leaves of plants to find the water it needs for survival.

Babies are easily sexed: Males can be identified by the tarsal spurs on their hinged legs.

Common Chameleon

Chamaeleo chameleon chameleon, Linnaeus, 1758: Beginner

Natural Distribution and Habitat
Distribution: Northern Africa, Southern Europe, Israel, Jordan, southwest Saudi Arabia, Yemen, Lebanon, Syria, Iraq, Iran.
Climate preference: Sudanese, Sudano-Guinean.
Forest stratum: Bushes, shrubs, small trees, cultivated zones, oases.

Breeding Data
Number of eggs per clutch: 15 to 40.
Number of clutches per year: 1.
Hatching time: 9 to 10 months at 77°F (25°C)
Sexual maturity: 8 months.
Life span: 5 years.
Maximum size: 12 inches.

Terrarium Care
Terrarium type: Sudanese
Notes: In my experience, this is a hardy, personable species of chameleon that needs two things to be bred and kept successfully in captivity: a diet enriched with iodine and a hibernating period. After a period of activity, hibernation can begin once the animals have been well fed. Hibernating chameleons can stay in a slightly moist, low-lit accommodation in a basement at 59°F (15°C) or even a hibernating box made out of Styrofoam and

with cooling equipment similar to that used for the cool incubation of eggs, for one and a half to two months. They are rather aggressive chameleons among themselves, and it is not recommended to keep them together. They are also notoriously cannibalistic and will eat small chameleons. Females will require a good feeding before being introduced to a potential mate. After copulation has occurred, gestation lasts for two months. The color of the eggs of this chameleon upon oviposition is orange, so do not discard them as being infertile or not properly calcified. Embryogenesis is kick-started after a quick cold torpor period (45 days at 74°F [24°C]); the eggs should then be left to incubate at 77–79°F (25–26°C) for about six months. Babies are hardy, but you will need to supplement the drinking water or food with a bit of iodine to keep them healthy.

Flap-necked Chameleon

Chamaeleo dilepis,
Leach, 1819: Beginner

Natural Distribution and Habitat
Distribution: Widespread all over eastern and southern Africa, with many subspecies and variations.
Climate preference: Forest edge, plateau, equatorial rainforest, and equatorial afromontane, depending on the origin of the animal.
Forest stratum: Mid-level, savanna.

Breeding Data
Number of eggs per clutch: 20 to 40.
Number of clutches per year: 1 to 2.
Hatching time: 10 months on average at temperatures varying from 72°F (22°C) to 80°F (27°C).
Sexual maturity: 9 months.
Life span: Over 2 years.
Maximum size: 13 inches (34 cm).

Terrarium Care
Terrarium type: Forest edge, plateau, equatorial rainforest, or equatorial afromontane, depending on the origin of the animal.
Notes: The main problem with the flap-necked chameleon comes from the fact that it is a very widespread type, covering many species living in very diverse environments, from mountainous rainforests to lowland savanna. If you are not able to determine the origin of your flap-necked chameleon, I suggest that you set up a cage with a mean average temperature of 75°F (24°C) and an RH of no less than 75 percent. Arrange for some thermal gradients (heat spots) and drier areas as you wish, and wait for a few days before making any changes to the setup. Flies are one of their favorite foods. Flap-necked chameleons make great pets; they can be very trusty animals and captive-bred specimens are always a joy to raise.

Crested Chameleon

Chamaeleo cristatus, Stutchbury, 1837: Intermediate

Natural Distribution and Habitat

Distribution: Western primary forests of Central Africa.
Climate preference: Equatorial rainforest, equatorial afromontane.
Forest stratum: Undergrowth forest, usually along streams.

Breeding Data

Number of eggs per clutch: 18 to 36.
Number of clutches per year: 1 to 2.
Hatching time: 7 months at temps fluctuating between 68°F (20°C) and 77°F (25°C), or 9 months at 73°F (23°C) constant.
Sexual maturity: 1 year.
Life span: Over 2 years.
Maximum size: 10 inches (25 cm).

Terrarium Care

Terrarium type: Equatorial rainforest, equatorial afromontane.
Notes: If you are thinking of keeping a chameleon in a paludarium (terrarium set up like a marsh) or in a terrarium with a small waterfall, the crested chameleon is the species of choice, as it has very high humidity requirements. Males (brown) are easily distinguished from the females (green). They are rather shy, and should live solitary lives except when breeding is meant to occur.

Chamaeleo calyptratus *(male).*

The male should be introduced into the cage of the female, and after the mating has taken place, the female should be left on her own again. She will remain gravid for three to four months. Eggs will be laid in a shallow tunnel dug under leaf litter (oak leaves recommended) and left to incubate at room temperature for nine months.

Helmeted Chameleon

Chamaeleo Hoehnelii, Steindachner, 1891: Intermediate

Natural Distribution and Habitat

Distribution: High-altitude forests of Kenya and Uganda.
Climate preference: Afro-alpine.

Chamaeleo hoehnelii *(female), Kenya type.*

at night, and the humidity in the air can rise as high as 100 percent. They wake up basking under the morning sun; then, once their preferred body temperature is reached, they go on a hunt for insects, with a predilection for flies. In captivity, this temperature drop at night is necessary to keep the animals at the peak of health, so you might need to make use of a cool box modeled on a cool incubator to put the animals to sleep. Males are notably aggressive to one another, whereas females can be housed communally.

Forest stratum: Shrubs and bushes, sometimes at mid-elevation in trees or forests.

Breeding Data
Number of babies per litter: 15 to 25.
Number of litters per year: 1 to 2.
Pregnancy: 5 months on average.
Sexual maturity: 5 months.
Life span: Over 2 years.
Maximum size: 10 inches (25 cm) for males.

Terrarium Care
Terrarium type: Afro-alpine.
Notes: These chameleons are found high up in the mountains, and one population is known to thrive at the border of Kenya and Uganda, on Mount Elgon, at 9,000 feet (3,000 m). There, they experience cool days and significantly cooler temperature

Sailfin Mountain Chameleon

Chamaeleo montium,
Buchholz, 1874: Beginner

Natural Distribution and Habitat
Distribution: Around Mount Cameroon and other mountains within Cameroon's Mamfe District.
Climate preference: Equatorial afromontane.
Forest stratum: Primary and secondary forests, shrubs and trees in gardens.

Breeding Data
Number of eggs per clutch: 8 to 15.
Number of clutches per year: 1 to 3.
Hatching time: 5 to 6 months at 72°F (22°C)
Sexual maturity: 6 months.

Chamaeleo deremensis *(male)*.

Life span: 2 years or so.
Maximum size: 10 inches (25 cm) for males, half that size for females.

Terrarium Care
Terrarium type: Equatorial afromontane.
Notes: The sailfin mountain chameleon does best at mild temperatures (71–79°F [22–26°C] daytime, 63–70°F [18–21°C] nighttime, and high humidity (80 percent daytime, 100 percent nighttime). They reproduce year round, with no specific mating season. Females lay from 5 to 11 eggs, two to three times a year. The gestation lasts for three months, and the babies will hatch from the eggs between five and six months if kept at a constant 72°F. Babies grow at a

moderate rate and might reach sexual maturity after six months if given insects laced with minerals and vitamins. I know of two morphs existing in the wild.

Usambara Three-horned Chameleon

Chamaeleo deremensis,
Matschie, 1892: Intermediate

Natural Distribution and Habitat
Distribution: Usambara Mountains in Tanzania, between 2,600 and 3,600 feet (800 to 1,100 m).

Climate preference: Equatorial afromontane.

Forest stratum: Primary forests, coffee plantations, shrubs and trees in gardens.

Breeding Data

Number of eggs per clutch: 20 to 35.

Number of clutches per year: 1

Hatching time: 5 months at 72°F (22°C) on average.

Sexual maturity: 10 months.

Life span: Over 3 years.

Maximum size: 12 inches (30 cm).

Terrarium Care

Terrarium type: Equatorial afromontane.

Notes: The males of this beautiful species of chameleon are adorned with three ringed horns, and both sexes show occipital lobes (small flaps on each side of the neck), a dorsal crest, and a short tail. They have high humidity requirements and can be rather shy with their keepers—hence the recommendation to house them in heavily planted terrariums. During the breeding season (once a year) females of this species will, at times, copulate with several males before laying large clutches of eggs (up to 50) after a gestation that usually spans just over 100 days. The babies are born aqua-blue, but this color soon fades away. The species experiences mild weather during the day (mid-70s F [20°C]) and cool and damp at night, with temperature drops of around 13°F (7°C).

Chamaeleo quadricornis *(male).*

Four-horned Chameleon

Chamaeleo quadricornis,
Tornier, 1899: Beginner

Natural Distribution and Habitat

Distribution: Mount Lefo and Manengouba in Cameroon, southeast Nigeria, 6,000–7,200 feet (1,700–2,200 m)

Climate preference: Equatorial afromontane, 70–82°F (21–28°C), 85–100% RH.

Forest stratum: Shrubs, more rarely found in remainders of primary forests.

Breeding Data

Number of eggs per clutch: 8 to 15.

Number of clutches per year: 2 to 3.

Hatching time: 5 to 6 months, incubating at a constant temperature of 72°F (22.5°C), or alternatively 77°F (25°C) degrees daytime and 64.4°F (18°C) nighttime.

Sexual maturity: 8 months.

Life span: 5 years.

Maximum size: Males 14 inches (35 cm), females are slightly smaller.

Terrarium Care

Terrarium type: Equatorial afromontane

Notes: This beautiful species of chameleon is at times available to the pet trade from Cameroonian exports. It has two subspecies: *C. quadricornis gracilior*, which is recognizable by its orange claws, and the nominate form, *C. quadricornis quadricornis*, which has gray claws. They inhabit the wet forest remains on the slopes of ancient volcanoes. Their very limited area of distribution makes them particularly vulnerable to heavy collection for the pet trade. They are, however, a rather easy species to maintain in captivity. They do have high humidity requirements, so a fogging system is recommended. In captivity, like many other mountainous species of chameleons, they tend to develop goiters that will fade away if the animals are given insects enriched with natural iodine (sea kelp). Babies are large when born and take over half a year to reach sexual maturity.

Giant Meller's Chameleon

Chamaeleo melleri,
Gray, 1864: Intermediate

Natural Distribution and Habitat

Distribution: Inland mountainous parts of Malawi, Tanzania, northern Mozambique, from sea level up to 3,300 feet (1,006 m).

Climate preference: Forest edge, 73–82°F (23–29°C). They take lower temperatures and RH (60%) in the day than in the nighttime—80–90%, 70–74°F (21–24°C).

Forest stratum: Tree canopy.

Breeding Data

Number of eggs per clutch: 30 to 80.

Number of clutches per year: 1 in the wild

Hatching time: 4 to 5 months at 77°F (25°C).

Sexual maturity: 2 years.

Life span: Over 10 years in captivity.

Maximum size: 2 feet (60 cm).

Terrarium Care

Terrarium type: Forest edge.

Notes: Meller's chameleons are a large species found along the coast of southern East Africa, frequently imported from Tanzania and occasionally from Mozambique. Very popular among hobbyists, they fare

Chamaeleo melleri.

better in a large enclosure or free-range room, and should not be encaged for too long of a time. They are territorial and routine animals, and usually roost on the same branch, defecate in the same place, come to bask under the same light, etc. This species is best left to dedicated keepers. They are choosy about their mates, and require quite a bit of a setup to feel at ease. Once a pair is established, they are best left together, as they bond strongly. It is a fast-growing species, and given that food and drinking water are supplemented daily with a vitamin-mineral mix, the babies will thrive in captivity.

For anyone keeping *C. melleri*, visiting the website of the great Katrina Francis is a must: *www.melleridiscovery.com*

Jackson's Chameleons

Chamaeleo jacksonii, jacksonii Boulenger, 1896; *Chamaeleo jacksonii merumontanus*, Rand, 1958; *Chamaeleo jacksonii xantholophus,* Eason, Ferguson, & Hebrard, 1998: Intermediate

Natural Distribution and Habitat
Distribution: Mountains of Kenya, Tanzania, and possibly eastern Uganda around and over 7,200 feet (2,200 meters). *C. j. xantholophus*

has been introduced in Hawaii, where a viable population lives at a lower altitude.

Climate preference: Equatorial afromontane, 74–82°F (24–28°C), 55% to 75% RH.

Forest stratum: Shrubs, coffee plantations, bushes in gardens, at times found in deep forested areas and pine trees.

Breeding Data
Number of babies per litter: 15 to 50, depending on the subspecies.
Number of litters per year: 1 to 2.
Pregnancy: 6 to 7 months on average.
Sexual maturity: 6 to 7 months.
Life span: Over 8 years in captivity (Bob Mailloux, personal observation).
Maximum size: 13 inches (35 cm).

Terrarium Care
Terrarium type: Equatorial afromontane
Notes: Three species (so far) of Jackson's chameleons have been described. While all male Jackson's are adorned with three horns (one rostral and two supraorbital), the females show neither (*C. j. xantholophus*), just one rostral (*C. j. merumontanus*), or three (*C. j. jacksonii*). Two types of Jackson's chameleons are currently available in the pet trade, the Yellow-Crested Jackson's chameleon, also found in Hawaii, and the imported Mount Meru Jackson's chameleon (*Chamaeleo jacksonii merumontanus*). The ideal

environment for the Yellow-Crested Jackson's (Chameleon *C. j. xantholophus*) has a 75 percent RH and a temperature range from 73°F (23°C) to a maximum of 82°F (28°C) during the day, and slightly less during the night (73°F). Unlike many other mountain chameleons, they have lower humidity requirements and will survive with a 55 percent RH during

Chamaeleo jacksonii.

the day for several weeks, provided that the RH gets higher during the night with a temperature drop. The males of the species *C. j. xantholophus* have been observed in Hawaii by Mary Lovein as guarding a harem of females.

Mount Meru Jackson's chameleons are a brightly colored smaller subspecies that need to be kept at cooler temperatures (68–73°F [20–23°C] day, 61°F [17°C] night); they also require a higher RH.

The food of these chameleons has to be supplemented daily with a mineral/vitamin mix as they have high requirements in antioxidants.

Johnston's Chameleon

Chamaeleo johnstoni, Boulenger, 1901: Beginner

Natural Distribution and Habitat

Distribution: Mountainous Forests of Burundi, East Congo, Rwanda, and Uganda, 3,330 to 8,200 feet (1,000–2,500 m) in altitude.

Climate preference: Equatorial afromontane, 74–82°F (24–28°C), 65% to 80% RH.

Forest stratum: Disturbed forests, forest galleries, primary forests.

Chamaeleo pardalis *(male) Ankaramy.*

Breeding Data

Number of eggs per clutch: 12 to 15.

Number of clutches per year: 1 to 2.

Hatching time: 3 months at 73°F (23°C), to 5 months at 70°F (21°C); sometimes 6 months at cooler incubating temperatures.

Sexual maturity: 8 months.

Life span: Over 2 years.

Maximum size: 10 inches (26 cm).

Terrarium Care

Terrarium type: Equatorial afromontane.

Notes: These chameleons have high humidity requirements, and depending on their origin, they might need to be kept at mild temperatures (Burundi) to cool temperatures (Uganda and Congo). They have a particular liking for snails and spiders, but they are not difficult or too demanding in their care. They usually are skittish animals. Johnston's chameleons, unlike the Jackson's, are egg-laying chameleons. Babies are born large, and the sex differentiation is easily made within a month after hatching as young males show some horns protruding, which are absent in females.

Dwarf East African Mountain Chameleons

Chamaeleo affinis, Rüppell, 1845;
Chamaeleo bitaeniatus Fisher, 1884,

Chamaeleo eliotti *(male).*

Chamaeleo elliotti, Günther, 1895;
Chamaeleo rudis, Boulenger, 1906:
Beginner

Natural Distribution and Habitat

Distribution: Mountainous parts of Ethiopia (*C. affinis*), Burundi, northeastern Congo, Kenya, Rwanda (*C.*

Captive bred **Furcifer antimena.**

Notes: These dwarf chameleon species require mild to cool temperatures (at night) and an RH from 60 to 85 percent. They are all ovoviviparous and will give birth to small chameleons. They can be accommodated with rather average-sized terrariums and can be kept in groups, as they are more social than most chameleons.

Labord's Chameleon

(the biological information for this species is identical to that of *Furcifer antimena*)
Furcifer labordi, Grandidier, 1872

Natural Distribution and Habitat

Distribution: Deciduous coastal forests of western Madagascar.

Climate preference: Forest edge, 75–82°F (24–28°C), 75% to 85% RH.

Forest stratum: Throughout the forest.

Breeding Data

Number of eggs per clutch: 8 to 12.

Number of clutches per year: 1.

Hatching time: 4 months at 79°F (26°C) and 2 weeks at 80°F (mostly males), 6 months at 74°F (24°C) then 15 days at 77°F (25°C) and another 2 weeks at 80°F (mostly females).

Sexual maturity: 3 months.

Life span: 2 years for the males.

ellioti), Sudan (*C. bitaeniatus*), Tanzania, Uganda (*C. rudis*), above 2,800 feet (800 m).

Climate preference: Equatorial afromontane, plateau, 70–82°F (21–28°C) daytime, lower at night; 65% to 100% RH daytime dry/rainy season, 60% to 100% nighttime dry/rainy season.

Forest stratum: Bushes and grasslands, sometimes found in trees and forests.

Breeding Data

Number of babies per litter: 8 to 20 depending on the species.

Number of litters per year: 1 to 3 depending on the species.

Pregnancy: 3 to 4 months for all the species.

Sexual maturity: 4 months.

Life span: 2 years.

Maximum size: 7 inches (15 cm).

Terrarium Care

Terrarium type: Equatorial afromontane, plateau.

Maximum size: 11 inches (28 cm) in some captive-bred specimens.

Terrarium Care
Terrarium type: Forest Edge
Notes: This surprising species is not available in the pet trade. Delicate, they will wither very quickly if not given the appropriate care, yet they grow as quickly as their cousins the carpet chameleons, whose nervousness and bright colors they share. Captive-bred specimens show some colors not seen in their wild counterparts, and although they are rather more placid, remain flighty. Individuals of both sexes need to be bred (or kept) apart for better chances of successful copulation. Females will quickly turn aggressive to their mates once the act is over, and they are better left in their own setup. They will take another couple of months before coming down to the soil and looking for a good place to lay their eggs. The substrate must be sandy or they will not dig into it. They might dig as deep as their total length, and unfortunately, usually die shortly after their unique oviposition.

Carpet Chameleon

Furcifer lateralis, Gray,
1851: Beginner

Natural Distribution and Habitat
Distribution: Central plateaus and southwest coast of Madagascar.

Furcifer lateralis *(female).*

Climate preference: Forest edge, plateau, Sudano-Guinean, 71–82°F (20–28°C), nighttime temperature drop necessary, 55% to 75% RH.
Forest stratum: Very diverse, from grass to tree canopy.

Breeding Data
Number of eggs per clutch: 12 to 16.
Number of clutches per year: 1 to 2.
Hatching time: 7 to 9 months (some clutches need a diapause to hatch); see Chapter 11.
Sexual maturity: 3 months.
Life span: 2 years.
Maximum size: 11 inches (28 cm) in *F. lateralis major* and some captive-bred specimens.

Terrarium Care

Terrarium type: Forest edge, plateau, Sudano-Guinean.

Notes: A small- to medium-sized, lively, nervous chameleon of which three morphs are known: Tananarive (Hauts Plateaux), Fort Dauphin, and Morondava. This species is fast-growing, and can reproduce at the tender age of three months. They are an adaptive species and show rather remarkable resilience to drought, cold, and even hot temperatures (high 80s) for a chameleon. In captivity, they are a typical heliophilic species, and love to bask under metal halides or morning sun. Breeding is easily achieved, but sexes and individuals are best kept separated, or at least in a large enclosure, so they might avoid one another.

Minor Chameleon

(the biological information for this species is identical to that of for *Furcifer petteri*)
F. minor, Günther, 1879

Natural Distribution and Habitat

Distribution: South central plateaus and forests of Madagascar.

Climate preference: Forest edge, plateau, subtropical afromontane, 71–82°F (20–28°C), 55% to 75% RH, temperatures can fall greatly in the night.

Forest stratum: Mid-elevation in vegetation. This species naturally occurs in Madagascar, but it is not being exported from the wild. It may sometimes be available from private keepers.

Breeding Data

Number of eggs per clutch: 8 to 12.

Number of clutches per year: 1.

Hatching time: 8 to 9 months at 73.5°F (23°C)

Sexual maturity: 8 months.

Life span: 2 years.

Maximum size: 12 inches (30 cm) for males, half that size for females.

Terrarium Care

Terrarium type: Plateau, subtropical afromontane.

Notes: After eight to nine months at a constant 73.5°F (23°C) and RH, *C. minor* babies are born to the world. They can already be identified as males or females from the presence or lack of budding horns. They take around eight months to reach adulthood, at which time the females will change from a uniform green to a flashy coloration, and the males will turn from green to shades of brick (orange, red, white, gray). Copulation in this species of chameleon is very easily obtained with healthy individuals. Once mated, the females display a striking new coloration, with a lot of black and become extremely aggressive to their mates, for which reason they need to be immediately parted after mating. Gestation usually lasts for two to three months, depending on the state of the animal. Females can be kept in groups as they will not attack one another, even if gravid, but

Furcifer minor.

need to be offered a food enriched with calcium and vitamins to ensure the viability of their egg production. In the wild, males generally outlive the females, who might die during or shortly after their first egg-laying experience. In captivity, it is possible to lessen the toll this takes on the females by ensuring good care and preventing exhaustion.

Panther Chameleon

Furcifer pardalis, Cuvier, 1829: Beginner

Natural Distribution and Habitat
Distribution: Coastal forests of northern Madagascar, Saint Paul, La Réunion Island.

Climate preference: Equatorial rainforest, forest edge, 74–90°F (24–29°C), 65% to 85% RH.
Forest stratum: Mid-elevation.

Breeding Data
Number of eggs per clutch: 20 to 40.
Number of clutches per year: 2 to 3.
Hatching time: 9 to 10 months (shorter incubations have been reported).
Sexual maturity: 6 to 8 months.
Life span: Over 6 years in captivity.
Maximum size: 22 inches (56 cm).

Terrarium Care
Terrarium type: Equatorial rainforest, forest edge.
Notes: Panthers combine many advantages in one chameleon: They are relatively large, they can be handled without too many precautions,

Technically, this species does not have any breeding season per say if kept under human care. After mating, the female will lay 20 to 30 eggs (rarely more) one month to 45 days later. Babies are sexable from the examination of the interstitial skin of their gular pouches: red in females, dark blue in males. The growth is rapid, and babies can be kept together and given more and more space as they grow. They require a diet enriched with vitamins and minerals for proper growth.

they are generally people-friendly (but not so to other chameleons, so beware!), and they are easily available in all kinds of colors, most of which are strikingly beautiful.

Giant Oustalet's Chameleon

Furcifer oustaleti, Moquard, 1894: Beginner

Natural Distribution and Habitat
Distribution: Widely distributed over the north and west of Madagascar, except for mountains and rainforests.
Climate preference: Sudanese, Sudano-Guinean, forest edge, plateau, 71–92°F (20–32°C), 40% to 75% RH.
Forest stratum: Small trees to canopy.

Breeding Data
Number of eggs per clutch: 30 to 60 eggs.

Furcifer oustaleti (female).

Number of clutch per year: 1 to 2.
Hatching time: 7 to 8 months at 81–82°F (27–28°C).
Sexual maturity: 10 months.
Life span: 5 years.
Maximum size: 2 feet (60 cm).

Terrarium Care

Terrarium type: Sudanese, Sudano-Guinean, forest edge, plateau
Notes: Care is similar to that of the Panther chameleons.

Spiny Chameleon

Furcifer verrucosus, Cuvier, 1829: Intermediate

Natural Distribution and Habitat

Distribution: Southwestern coastal region of Madagascar.
Climate preference: Sudanese, Sudano-Guinean, forest edge, 71–79°F (20–29°C), 50% to 75% RH.
Forest stratum: Small trees, thickets, bushes.

Breeding Data

Number of eggs per clutch: 30 to 40.
Number of clutches per year: 1.
Hatching time: 7 to 8 months.
Sexual maturity: 8 to 10 months.
Life span: 4 years.
Maximum size: 20 inches (50 cm).

Terrarium Care

Terrarium type: Sudanese, Sudano-Guinean, forest edge.

Notes: Care is similar to that of the Panther chameleons, except for the fact that these chameleons take lower temperatures and RH.

Fischer's Chameleons

Three species fall under the denomination of Fischer's chameleons: *K. fischeri, Kinyongia multituberculata,* and *K. uluguruensis.* The care is almost identical for all of them.
K. multituberculata Reichenow, 1895: Intermediate

Natural Distribution and Habitat

Distribution: Lush plateaus and mountain forests of Kenya and Tanzania.
Climate preference: Equatorial afromontane, 71–80°F (20–26°C), 65% to 90% RH.
Forest stratum: Mid-elevation.

Breeding Data

Number of eggs per clutch: 14 to 20.
Number of clutches per year: 1 to 2.
Hatching time: 9 months at 73.5°F (23°C), 1 month at 77°F (25°C).
Sexual maturity: 8 months.
Life span: 3 years.
Maximum size: 15 inches (38 cm).

Terrarium Care

Terrarium type: Equatorial afromontane.

Kinyongia multituberculata.

Notes: *Kinyongia multituberculata* is the most common Fischer's Chameleon in the pet trade. It is a medium-sized animal. Males and females are strongly dimorphic, the females showing just the presence of horn buds instead of long *canthi rostralis* (the two elongated, flattened horns projecting over the nostrils). These mountain chameleons can be found in open savannas, at the edges of forests, and in gardens and orchards. Gestation lasts for around two months, during which time the females will show a hearty appetite. Eggs are laid in a burrow 4 to 8 inches deep.

Rainforest Malagasy Stump-tailed Chameleons

Brookesia species (*Br. minima, Br. betschi, Br. superciliaris,*): Beginner

Natural Distribution and Habitat

Distribution: Eastern forest and several mountainous areas in Madagascar.

Climate preference: Tropical rainforest, subtropical afromontane, daytime 73–79°F (23–26°C), 80% RH, temperatures diminish little during the night.

Forest stratum: Ground to several feet up from the ground.

Breeding Data
Number of eggs per clutch: 2 to 4.
Number of clutches per year: 1 to 2.
Hatching time: 2 months-plus on average.
Sexual maturity: 6 months in artificial environment.
Life span: 2 years.
Maximum size: 2.8 inches (7 cm) for *Brookesia superciliaris.*

Terrarium Care
Terrarium type: Tropical rainforest, subtropical afromontane.
Notes: These species can be given a two-month cool resting period in the winter; the RH should not drop below 70 percent.

Climate preference: Forest Edge 74–82°F (23.5–28°C), 75% RH during the active season; 68–74°F (20–23.5°C), 40% RH during the dry and cool season (be sure to provide hiding spots for them); 75–86°F (24–30°C), 35% RH during the hot and dry season (the animals will stay underground, and come out when the humidity rises).
Forest stratum: Ground and thickets.

Breeding Data
Number of eggs per clutch: 2 to 3, rarely more.
Number of clutches per year: 1 to 2.
Hatching time: 2 months on average at 77°F (25°C).
Sexual maturity: 7 to 8 months in artificial environment.
Life span: Over 2 years.
Maximum size: Depends on the species.

Dry Forest Malagasy Stump-tailed Chameleons

Brookesia species (*Br. decaryi, Br. stumpffi*): Intermediate

Natural Distribution and Habitat
Distribution: Western and northern Madagascar.

Brookesia decaryi *(female).*

Rhampholeon viridis *(male)*.

Terrarium Care

Terrarium type: Forest edge.

Notes: Providing some ground cover is a must if you decide to replicate the seasonal changes for these chameleons. They will go into hiding niches in the ground and considerably slow down their metabolic activity with lower humidity. They will emerge from their hiding spots as soon as they feel the RH is high enough for their normal activities.

Rhampholeon spinosum.

East African Pygmy Leaf Chameleon

Rhampholeon species (*R. acuminatum, R. viridis, R. spinosum*): Intermediate. (The care information for this species also applies to *Brookesia vadoni, Calumma fallax, C. gallus, C. gastrotaenia, C. nasuta*)

Natural Distribution and Habitat

Distribution: Mountains of East Africa.

Climate preference: Subtropical afromontane.

Forest stratum: Ground to lower branches.

Breeding Data

Number of eggs per clutch: 2 to 7.

Number of clutches per year: Unknown.

Hatching time: A bit over 2 months at 71.6°F (22°C)

Sexual maturity: Unknown.

Life span: Unknown.

Maximum size: 4 inches (6 cm) and over (*R. spinosum*).

Terrarium Care

Terrarium type: Subtropical afromontane.

Notes: These chameleons need to go through a dormant period of a couple of months during the winter. The daily temperatures fall to 63°F (17°C) in the day, and the mid-50s°F

(13°C) at night. They will turn black and stop eating. This dormancy period is necessary to induce breeding in these species.

Twig Pygmy Chameleon

Rieppeleon kerstenii, Peters, 1868: Beginner

Natural Distribution and Habitat
Distribution: Kenya, Somalia, Tanzania.
Climate preference: Forest edge, plateau.
Forest stratum: Grass and remains of forests.

Breeding Data
Number of eggs per clutch: 5 to 10.
Number of clutches per year: 2.
Hatching time: 2 months, on average at 77°C (25°C).
Sexual maturity: 7 to 8 months.
Life span: 2 years.
Maximum size: 2 inches (5 cm).

Terrarium Care
Terrarium type: Forest edge, plateau.
Notes: A hardy, adaptable species.

Usambara Pygmy Chameleon

Rieppeleon brevicaudatus, Matschie, 1892: Beginner

Rhampholeon kerstenii (female).

Natural Distribution and Habitat
Distribution: Usambara Mountains, Tanzania.
Climate preference: Equatorial afromontane.
Forest stratum: Undergrowth forests.

Breeding Data
Number of eggs per clutch: 2 to 4.
Number of clutches per year: 2 to 3.
Hatching time: 2 months.
Sexual maturity: 8 months.
Life span: 2 years.
Maximum size: 2 inches (5 cm).

Terrarium Care
Terrarium type: Equatorial afromontane.
Notes: Robust and recommended for beginners.

Useful Addresses and Literature

Publications

Books
Peter Nečas, *Chameleons: Nature's Hidden Jewels, 2nd Edition*. Malabar, Florida: Krieger Pub. Co., 1999.

Peter Nečas and Wolfgang Schmidt, *Stump-tailed Chameleons: Miniature Dragons of the Rainforest*. Frankfurt, Germany: Edition Chimaira, 2004.

Periodicals
Reptiles Magazine
http://www.reptilechannel.com

Reptilia Magazine
http://www.reptilia.net/html_english/index.htm

Web Pages
AdCham
(Famous website on chameleons)
www.adcham.com

Chameleons! E-zine
(A chameleon E-zine. Great articles)
www.chameleonnews.com/index.html

Chameleons-online!
http://chamaeleons-online.com/

Chameleon Forums
(General forum about chameleons. Great for contacts and links to breeders, suppliers, etc.)
http://www.chameleonforums.com/

Chameleons, general
(A source of inspiration for chameleons)
http://www.chameleonsonline.com/

Classifieds
www.kingsnake.com
www.faunaclassifieds.com

Jackson's Chameleons (Everything about Jackson's chameleons)
http://www.geocities.com/chamjacksonii/

Jackson's Chameleons in Hawaii
(Jackson's chameleons in the
Hawaiian wild)
http://www.lovein.com/JacknJill.html

Meller's Chameleons
(A great website dedicated to
Meller's chameleons)
http://www.melleridiscovery.com

Panther chameleons
(Panthers are very popular
chameleons for hobbyists.
Find out more here)
http://chamworld.blogspot.com/

Veiled Chameleons
(Great blog about Veiled chameleons)
*http://raisingkittytheveiledchameleon.
blogspot.com*

Equipment and Electronics

Cool Incubators
www.kassiba.com

Live Food
Silkworms Canada
www.canadiansilkworms.com

Silkworms USA
www.silkwormwholesale.com

Hornworms and other
www.carolinapetsupply.com

Nutritional Complements
Miscellaneous
www.carolinapetsupply.com

Astaxanthin
www.kassiba.com

Glossary

Acrodont: a formation of the teeth whereby the teeth are consolidated with the summit of the alveolar ridge of the jaw without sockets. The term also refers to species of reptiles that have such a formation.

Aestivation: also known as "summer sleep." A state of dormancy somewhat similar to hibernation. It takes place during times of heat and dryness, the hot dry season, which is often but not inevitably, the summer months.

Akynesis: reflex transient immobility, in animals "playing dead" to avoid predators.

Allantois: egg membrane that becomes the urine and waste receptacle for the embryo.

Arboreal: primarily tree or shrub dwelling.

Bicuspid: cleft or having two ending points. The nails of some stumptailed chameleons are biscuspid.

Biomes: a regional ecosystem characterized by distinct types of vegetation and animals that have developed under specific geo-climatic conditions.

Biorhythm: physiological cycle.

Biotope: an area uniform in its environmental parameters, supporting its own species of plants and animals.

Brumation: a hibernation-like state that cold-blooded animals utilize during very cold weather.

Carolus Linnaeus: also known as Carl von Linné. A Swedish botanist, 1707–1778, who was the first naturalist to classify the plants or Earth in an orderly arrangement.

Chalaza: fibrous ligament that always returns the bird embryo to its original position when the egg is rolled over.

Chromatophore: pigment-containing and light-reflecting cells found in amphibians, fish, reptiles, crustaceans, and cephalopods. They are largely responsible for generating skin and eye color in cold-blooded animals. They are generated in the neural crest during embryonic development.

Circadian: an approximate daily periodicity. A roughly-24-hour cycle in the biochemical, physiological or behavioral processes of living beings, including plants, animals, fungi, and cyanobacteria.

Cloaca: external opening at the base of the tail, which is shared by the urinary, digestive, and reproductive systems.

Cold torpor: state of decreased physiological activity in an animal, usually characterized by a reduced body temperature and rate of metabolism.

Conduction: the spontaneous transfer of thermal energy through matter, from a region of higher temperature to a region of lower temperature, and acts to equalize temperature differences. It is also described as heat energy transferred from one material to another by direct contact.

Cone cell: photoreceptor cells lodged on the retina of the eye. Cone cells are wavelength sensitive and depending on the cell, might pick up a certain range of wavelength and not another.

Convection: transfer of thermal energy within the same fluid (air or water) creating a current as it moves from one place to another (usually upwards) as it warms up.

Deciduous: forest made up of trees that shed their leaves during the dry season to save water.

Dehydration: lack of water.

Diapause: a physiological state of dormancy with very specific triggering and releasing conditions. It is used as a means to survive predictable, unfavorable environmental conditions, such as temperature extremes, drought, or reduced food availability.

Diurnal: Day active.

Dorsal: referring to the back of the body; along the spine.

Endemic: native to one region only.

Eurytropic: able to adapt to a wide range of environmental conditions; widely distributed.

Evaporation: the slow vaporization of a liquid and the reverse of condensation. A type of phase transition, it is the process by which molecules in a liquid state (e.g. water) spontaneously become gaseous (e.g. water vapor).

Gravid: said of females containing developing eggs.

Gular crest: modified scales that hang down from the throat in one or two rows.

Heliophilic: sun-loving.

Hemipenis (plural hemipenes): copulating organ in male squamates (lizards and snakes).

Hybrids: individuals produced from parents with different numbers of chromosomes. Hybrids can give birth to fertile offspring.

Insectivorous: diet consisting of insects.

Jacobson's organ: an auxiliary olfactory sense organ that is found in many animals. It was discovered by Ludvig Jacobson in 1813.

Microclimate: a local atmospheric zone where the climate differs from the surrounding area. The term may refer to areas as small as a few square feet (for example a garden bed) or as large as many square miles (for example a valley).

Morphology: study of the structures and shapes of animals.

Mycotic infection: Fungal, parasitic infection.

Occipital lobe: Skin flap extending from the back of the head onto the neck.

Oogenesis: egg formation.

Oviparous: egg-laying.

Oviposition: action for a female to deposit her eggs.

Ovoviviparous: species in which the eggs remain in the oviduct and are expulsed when the babies are ready to be born. Ovoviviparous species do not have a real placenta like viviparous species do.

Pathogen: disease causing agent.

Pineal gland: a small endocrine gland in the vertebrate brain. It produces melatonin, a hormone that affects the modulation of wake/sleep patterns and photoperiodic (seasonal) functions.

Poikilotherm: a living organism whose body temperature follows that of its environment. In other words, it is dependent on its environment to provide for its body temperature.

Polarized: a state or a process by which rays of light exhibit different properties and scatter in different directions.

Prehensile: able to grab with and to maintain a grip.

Radiation: any process in which energy emitted by one body travels through a medium or through space, ultimately to be absorbed by another body.

Rostrums: nasal projections.

Sciophilous: shade-loving.

Sexual dimorphism: standard differences in shapes, sizes, and colorations between sexes.

Species: one of the basic units of biological classification and a taxonomic rank. A species is often defined as a group of organisms capable of interbreeding and producing fertile offspring.

Subspecies: the taxonomic rank immediately subordinate to a species. A subspecies is a taxonomic group which is less distinct than the primary stock or species from which it originates. The characteristics attributed to subspecies are generally derived from changes that have taken place or evolved as a result of geographical distribution or isolation from the primary species or *nominate form*, also called nominate subspecies.

Tegument: a cluster of nonessential and essential proteins that line the space between the envelope and nucleocapsid of many enveloped viruses. The tegument generally contains proteins that aid in viral replication and evasion of the immune response, typically with inhibition of the signaling and activation of interferon.

Thermoregulation: action of regulating one's body temperature.

UVA: said of electromagnetic wavelengths between 315 and 400 nanometers. Many animals (including chameleons) have cone cells sensitive to UVA and parts of their teguments are specifically reflective to UVA for peer-to-peer signalization.

UVB: electromagnetic wavelengths comprised between 290 and 315 nanometers. UVB are more energetic than UVA and penetrate more deeply into the skin of the animals. Their photosynthetic action turns the precursor of the vitamin D found in the fat tissues of the skin into vitamin D.

UVC: the last group of UV rays, also the most energetic one, ranging from 200 to 290 nanometers. UVC are used for their germicidal properties in air and water treatment. Mercury vapor lamps emit UVC that are harmful to the eyes and may cause eye burn in humans and animals.

Variation: a morphological or physiological difference (generally observed in a given population but also in individual animals) from the recognized norm or nominate form.

Xeric: hot and dry.

Index

Spiny chameleon, 141
Sprinkling systems, 59
Stillbirths, 102–103
Stomatitis, 114
Stress, 53–54
Stump-tailed chameleons, 11–12, 21, 142–144
Subcutaneous injections, 117
Subfamilies, 5–6
Subspecies, 1
Substrate, 98–100
Sudanese terrarium, 75–76, 78, 103
Sudano-Guinean terrarium, 75–76, 103
Sunlight, 59–60

T
Tail, 27
Tapeworms, 111
Taxonomy, 2–6
Terrariums. *See also specific species*
  cage vs., 68–69
  egg incubation temperature, 103
  heating of, 72
  lighting, 70–71
  relative humidity in, 72–73
  size of, 69
  types of, 75–79
Territoriality, 38–39
Thermoregulation, 25–26, 38, 42
Time mating, 96
Toes, 26
Tongue, 29, 34

Trematodes, 111–112
Tropical rainforest terrarium, 75–76, 79
Trypanosomiasis, 109
Twig Pygmy chameleon, 145
Tyndall effect, 36–37

U
Ultrasonic humidifiers, 73
Ultraviolet radiation, 22, 57–58, 64
Uric acid, 35
Urinary system, 32–33
Usambara Pygmy chameleon, 145
Usambara Three-horned chameleon, 129–130

V
Variations, 1–2
Veiled chameleon, 52–53, 124–125
Ventilation, 74
Vermiculite, 100, 101
Veterinarian, 107
Viruses, 108
Visual examination, 118
Vitamin D, 57, 60
Vitamins, 80–81, 113–114
Volcanic soil, 99–100

W
Water, 66–67, 81
Watering systems, 59, 61
Waxworms, 90–91

X
X-rays, 118